The Professional Programmers Guide to
Prolog

The Professional Programmers Guide to

Prolog

Alan G Hamilton
Department of Computing Science
University of Stirling

Pitman

PITMAN PUBLISHING
128 Long Acre, London WC2E 9AN

A Division of Longman Group UK Limited

© Alan G Hamilton 1989

First published in Great Britain 1989

British Library Cataloguing in Publication Data
Hamilton, A. G. (Alan G.)
  Professional programmers guide to PROLOG. –
  (Professional programmers guides).
  1. Computer systems. Programming languages: PROLOG
  I. Title II. Series
  005.13'3

ISBN 0 273 02854 5

Printed and bound in Great Britain at
The Bath Press, Avon

Contents

Contents

Preface

It is often said that once you have learned to use one programming language, you have learned them all. Of course this is not literally true, but learning to *program* does seem to be a side-effect of learning to use any one particular language, so that learning to use another language subsequently is appreciably easier. In this book I assume that the reader has some programming experience in some language. The book is not, therefore, about programming as such. But Prolog is different in kind from all other languages. It is structured differently, its semantics have a different form, and its execution is by a process which seems to have more to do with logic than with computation. These differences can be daunting to a newcomer to Prolog, and it does require time and experience (and perseverance) to become accustomed to them.

This book is intended to be a straightforward introduction for someone who wishes to gain a facility with Prolog. It is not about the theoretical basis of the language. It is about how to use it. It is not about any particular applications area. But it recognises the need for practical exercise when learning a new language.

Nevertheless, the book has two distinct aims: first, to be a tutorial introduction, and second, to be a reference for the basic Prolog facilities. The first six chapters are primarily intended to serve the first purpose, being an introduction to the Prolog interpreter and what to do to make it work. Chapters 7 to 19 retain this flavour, but are more clearly focused on particular features of Prolog. The final two chapters contain a large number of examples and solutions. These are intended to serve both as exercises for the reader and as illustrations of actual Prolog code. The appendices are purely for reference purposes. The more substantial is Appendix A, which contains an alphabetical list of built-in facilities with a brief description of each.

It is an unfortunate fact that there is no such thing as *standard* Prolog. There are many (increasingly many) different implementations of Prolog available. Naturally their authors have sought to include particular features or modifications which seem to them to be desirable. The result is quite a lot of confusion and incompatibility. I have not attempted to be encyclopaedic — it would be a huge task to describe all the variations which exist. In any case that would detract from my purpose, which is to provide a book from which a reader can easily learn the essentials of the language. So here you will find what might be regarded as the basic features only, with occasional references to alternative forms or additional features. I have tried to indicate which parts are completely standard, and where variations are likely to occur. It is perhaps worth mentioning in particular that micro-Prolog, which is a popular version of Prolog for microcomputers, is substantially different from what is described in this book. It is based on the same principles, but its syntax makes it, in appearance at least, a different language. Similar comments apply to Turbo Prolog.

There is a great deal of interest currently in Prolog, particularly in respect of the so-called *fifth generation* of computer languages. I do not wish to claim that Prolog is the best programming language. That would be absurd. I shall not even claim that it is the best language for any particular application, for that depends on the criteria by which one judges 'the best'. But it does have advantages over other languages in certain respects. Complex programs can be very short, and yet (to the experienced reader) still very clear. Applications which require the storage and manipulation of information about *relationships* fit particularly well with the way that Prolog represents and operates on data. And the connection of Prolog with logic makes it appropriate for applications in which some form of inference process plays a part, such as expert systems. Prolog is a different way of programming, which opens up new ideas and new possibilities. When you know it, you will find it an interesting and rewarding tool.

There are some acknowledgements which I wish to make. Phil Collier's excellent notes on Prolog were my original stimulus to explore this new and different approach to programming. His evangelism made me into a convert. Andrew Ireland read an entire draft of this book and made several suggestions for improvement. Ian Wilson has been a valuable source of ideas, with his constant probing into the awkwardnesses of Prolog. It was with encouragement from him that I embarked on this project, and I am grateful for his numerous comments and suggestions. Finally, the book was prepared using LaTeX on an Olivetti/AT&T 3B15 machine owned by the Department of Computing Science at the University of Stirling. Thanks are due to the Department and to the University, but particularly to Sam Nelson, for his patience both with his machines and with their users.

AGH
November 1988

1 Getting Started

Prolog is different. You will take some time to get used to it, as it requires its own distinctive way of thinking. Most people find it difficult at first, but after a while reach a point where it 'clicks', and from then on it becomes an interesting and rewarding language with which to work. So persevere! This volume is intended to help you to reach that point. It is not about the difficult and advanced techniques of Prolog, still less is it about the theoretical background – it is about getting used to Prolog's ways, so that you may in due course explore the intricacies yourself.

We begin with how Prolog appears to the user sitting at a terminal. So this first chapter is intended to be read while at a terminal, experimenting.

Prolog is more than a language. It is a language with an interpreter. In fact any computer language is useless without a compiler or an interpreter which give the various instructions in the language actual meanings or effects. The existence of such semantics in the case of Prolog is very apparent to the user for two reasons – first because the user interacts directly (step by step) with the interpreter, and second because the language is designed to work in an unusual way.

Now let us suppose that you are at a terminal and have called the Prolog interpreter. In most cases this is done by means of a command 'prolog', but you may have to check your particular system to find out the appropriate command. Now is perhaps as good a time as any to note also how to exit from Prolog. In most cases CTRL-Z (end-of-file) will take you out. But again this may be system-dependent. Other possible ways out are to key in **end.** or **halt.** When you enter Prolog, the interpreter gives a prompt, which will be (or will include) **?-**, and waits for you to respond. You can do only one sort of thing in response to the prompt, and that is to give a *goal* to the interpreter. This goal is not a command, nor is it an instruction. As the name suggests, it is something which the interpreter will set out to *achieve*. There is a standard form for goals, but the effects caused by trying to achieve them can be very different.

Let us try some goals. The following all include the **?-**, in order to indicate that they are goals, but you should omit this when keying them in. The first group are very simple goals which cause no surprises. Be sure

1

to enter the full stop at the end of each (if by mistake you press RETURN before the full stop, just key in the full stop on the next line, followed by another RETURN). Try the following seven goals (separately). You will see that after each one the interpreter will respond with a message, and may wait for you to press RETURN again before returning to the ?- prompt ready for the next goal.

```
?- write('Hello user!').
?- write(1987).
?- 2 < 3.
?- 3 < 2.
?- not(3 < 2).
?- 5 = 5.
?- 5 = X.
```

The last is the only one which requires comment. Here X is a Prolog variable (as is any upper case letter). This goal can be achieved by giving the value 5 to X, so this is what the interpreter does. The message which appears on the screen may show this value for X either explicitly with X = 5, or implicitly with 5 = 5. After this the interpreter waits for you to key in RETURN before allowing you to proceed. This is our first experience of variables in Prolog, so it is an appropriate place to give a warning. Variables behave in an unusual way in Prolog. In particular there are no global variables (all variables are in effect parameters of one kind or another), and there is no such thing as assignment. More about this later.

A goal which is achieved by the interpreter is said to *succeed*. A goal which is not achieved is said to *fail*. Examples of both occur in the list you have just tried. Note the different forms of response which the interpreter gives. Now let us move on to some goals which involve computation. The first two are what might be described as 'false starts'.

```
?- 2 + 3.
```

This doesn't get us anywhere. It is an inappropriate form for a goal. A goal is something which may turn out to be true or false (although there are exceptions, like goals involving write, as above).

```
?- X = 2 + 3.
```

Surprisingly, perhaps, this doesn't get us very far either. This goal is achieved by giving X the value 2 + 3. But 2 + 3 is a formal expression and as such (according to Prolog) is different from 5.

```
?- X is 2 + 3.
```

At last, this is what we are looking for. X is now given the value 5.

```
?- Y is (4 + 2) * 3.
?- R is 4 + 2 * 3.
```

The 'reserved word' is causes evaluation of arithmetic expressions.

Next we can explore ways in which more complicated goals can be formed.

```
?- write('Hello'), write(' user'), write('!').
?- write('Hello'), nl, write('How are you?').
```

Note the effect of the goal nl. It causes the next write to output on the next line.

```
?- X is 2 + 3, write(X).
?- P = 117, V is P * 2, write('Value: '), write(V).
```

So this is the way we write sequences of goals. Just separate them by commas, and the interpreter takes each in turn. Note the way in which variables are used as parameters. In the first goal, X is first given a value, and then the value is passed to write. In the second, the value P * 2 is computed, then given to V and finally passed to write.

There is also another way to combine goals. Goals can be given as alternatives, in effect combined by 'or'. Prolog uses the semicolon for this (where in the previous two goals the comma in effect means 'and').

```
?- write('Hello'); write(' user!').
?- X is 2 + 3; write(X).
```

In each of these cases the compound goal is achieved as soon as the first part is achieved, so the second part is ignored.

```
?- 3 < 2; write('Wrong!').
```

This succeeds – the first part fails, but then the second part succeeds. A goal involving write always succeeds.

Next, try these:

```
?- old(methuselah).
?- father(adam,cain).
?- greaterthan(3,2).
?- positive(X * X + 1).
```

All of these receive the 'thumbs down' from the interpreter. It cannot achieve them. The reason for this is that it does not have any information about the terms used, namely old, father, greaterthan, positive. These words make sense to us, and we can imagine easily what are the questions which are being asked when we give these goals. But to the Prolog interpreter they have no meaning at all. (We shall see later how we can arrange for the interpreter to 'know' about such things). It does know about write, is, +, *, =, <, and various other basic 'built-in' facilities, and so was able to interpret goals which involved these sensibly. One of the features of Prolog is that there is no such response as 'don't know'. If Prolog doesn't know then it responds with no. The response yes means 'I can achieve this'. The response no means 'I cannot achieve this'. Be careful to remember that the latter embraces both 'This is false' and 'I don't know whether this is true or false'.

Now we have established that the Prolog interpreter doesn't know very much. It comes stocked only with a limited supply of information about certain basic constructs (like those listed above). In order for users to carry out their own tasks there are ways to augment the information known to the interpreter. The system has space for a database which is available to the user. It does not have a name, and we shall refer to it throughout merely as *the database*. To store something in the database we first give the goal

```
?- [user].
```

Remember that the interpreter accepts goals only. The response to this goal is that the interpreter waits for you to enter data. It may give a prompt, or it may not. Try keying in exactly the following:

```
old(john).
old(jane).
young(bill).
```

Follow these by CTRL-Z (or your system end-of-file, or on some systems ?- end., here including the ?-). This then returns you to the ?- prompt, meaning that your data has been stored, and the interpreter is ready to accept the next goal. The database now contains three facts, two about old and one about young. The words old and young here are *predicates*, which means that they are used to represent properties. For example, the term old(jane) is to be regarded as the assertion 'jane is old'. The words john, jane and bill are *names*, and as such they are constants, not variables. For the time being we shall use only single upper-case letters for variables. See Chapters 10 and 11 for details of the distinction between constants and variables. Try the following goals:

4

```
?- old(jane).
?- young(jane).
?- old(X).
```

Each time the interpreter is simply checking the goal as given against the data stored in the database. Note that the goal containing a variable is achieved by choosing a value which causes the goal to match a known 'fact'. There may be alternative values (as there are here, because there are two facts about old). In this situation the interpreter scans the database in order, and chooses the first fact which matches. It follows that the order in which facts are held in the database is significant.

Now give the goal

```
?- [user].
```

again, and enter the line

```
wiser(X,Y) :- old(X), young(Y).
```

Remember to include the full stop! Return to the interpreter as before. The database has now been extended. But this time the information we have inserted is rather different. Think of the symbol :- as meaning 'if', and the comma as meaning 'and'. See what happens when you try the goals

```
?- wiser(jane,bill).
?- wiser(jane,john).
?- wiser(john,Z).
```

Besides the facts about old and young, the database now contains a general rule, which specifies certain circumstances in which two objects are to satisfy the predicate wiser. (Notice that a predicate can express a property of any number of objects, not just of a single object, as old and young did. The term wiser(jane,bill) is intended to mean 'jane is wiser than bill'.)

This may be taken further. Extend the database again (by the same procedure) so that it contains also

```
dark_haired(john).
grey_haired(jane).
dark_haired(bill).
wiser(X,Y) :- grey_haired(X), dark_haired(Y).
```

Next try the goal

```
?- wiser(jane,john).
```

5

Where the answer previously had been **no**, the extra information now means that this goal can be achieved. Note that there is no difficulty associated with having two (or more) rules associated with the predicate **wiser**. They complement each other.

The examples so far illustrate the basic processes which the interpreter uses. But there is rather more to it, as we shall see in the ensuing chapters. For the last example of this chapter, though, let us introduce something a little more substantial. Try the goal

```
?- wiser(X,Y).
```

The interpreter will achieve this in the first way it can, finding values for X and Y in the process. It will find the rule which says

```
wiser(X,Y) :- old(X), young(Y).
```

It will then achieve old(X) in the first way it can, i.e. with X = john. Then it will proceed to achieve young(Y) in the first way it can, i.e. with Y = bill. Thus these are the values chosen to achieve the goal ?- wiser(X,Y).

Remember that ':-' means 'if', and ',' means 'and'. Try for yourself entering further information into the database, and then giving further goals to the interpreter. If the interpreter doesn't understand something it may give a message including [break]. If this happens, try CTRL-Z (end-of-file), and you should return to the ?- prompt. (More than one CTRL-Z may be necessary.)

There are some points to note about using the database in this way.

1. The facts and rules for a particular predicate currently held in the database may be displayed on the screen by means of the built-in facility **listing**. For example, try the goals

   ```
   ?- listing(old).
   ?- listing(wiser).
   ```

2. When you exit from Prolog the contents of the database are lost completely. Remember this! We shall see later how to save information in a file.

3. Although extending the database is easy, as we have seen, changing something previously entered, or recovering from problems caused by entering something erroneously, can be awkward. If you do get in mess doing this, the most convenient way to recover may be to exit from Prolog altogether and start again from scratch. At any time you can use **listing** to see the contents of the database.

4. There are other ways of managing the contents of the database which are more practical. The procedure given above should not be used except for small-scale or demonstration purposes. See Chapter 5 and Chapter 15.

Let us end this introduction with a discussion of some standard Prolog terminology. We have seen that the 'achievement' of a goal can happen in one of a number of ways. Some goals (like those involving `write`) are achieved immediately. Others are achieved immediately, but by the process of identifying the goal as a known fact. Others require the more complicated process of using a rule. Further, the achievement of a goal can result in variables being given values. Perhaps unfortunately, it is standard practice among Prolog users to use terminology which confuses these distinctions. To say that a goal is *satisfied* or is *proved* is the same as saying that it is achieved. We shall often adopt this usage, too, in the remainder of this book.

2 Facts, Rules and Goals

Let us now be more precise about the forms of expression which we have been using. First, what exactly is a goal? Informally, when we give a goal to the interpreter we may think of it as a question. The question asks whether a certain assertion is true (or, if it contains variables, whether it can be satisfied by some choice of values). The word *predicate* is used to mean an assertion which may be true or false, and which may have parameters (standing for objects about which an assertion is being made).

Formally, in its simplest form a goal consists of the symbol ?- followed by a single expression (i.e. a predicate, which may or may not have arguments), followed by a full stop.

In a *compound* goal the single expression is replaced by a combination of such expressions constructed by means of the comma ('and') and the semicolon ('or').

The Prolog interpreter can deal only with goals. That is why the ?- appears in the prompt, and need not be input by the user. But we have seen also *facts* and *rules* in Chapter 1. The database can contain facts and rules (and only facts and rules).

A fact consists of a single expression (as in a goal) followed by a full stop. Examples are

```
old(john).
father(adam,cain).
forebear(adam,X).
```

Notice that facts may contain variables. (Remember that names in lower-case letters are constants, and upper-case letters are variables.) Notice also that, formally at least, the only way that a goal is distinguished from a fact is by the prefix ?-.

Next, a rule consists of

1. the *head* of the rule, which is a single expression (as in a goal or a fact).

2. the symbol :-, which may be read as 'if'.

3. the *body* of the rule, which may be either a single expression or a combination of single expressions constructed by means of commas and semicolons (as in a compound goal).

4. a full stop.

Examples of rules are:

```
wiser(X,Y) :- old(X), young(Y).
write_prompt :- write('Enter first number: ').
parent(X,Y) :- father(X,Y); mother(X,Y).
grandparent(X,Y) :- parent(X,Z), parent(Z,Y).
```

Facts and rules in the database are the 'knowledge' that the Prolog interpreter can use when trying to achieve goals. This knowledge usually forms a kind of hierarchy of dependence. For example, the rule about **grandparent** given above will be useless unless the interpreter knows about the predicate **parent**, and likewise the rule about **parent** depends on facts or rules about **father** and **mother**.

Rules almost always contain variables. We shall leave detailed discussion of variables until later, but there is a point worth making here. Variables which appear in the head of a rule may appear anywhere in the body of the rule – these are analogous to parameters in a procedure in (say) Pascal. But some variables may occur in the body of a rule and not in the head – these are analogous to *local* variables in a Pascal procedure. For example, the variable Z in the **grandparent** rule above is one of these 'local' variables. Once an application of such a rule is completed, all such local variables are forgotten. Remember this!

Now let us look at how the interpreter interprets. It has a body of built-in information and it may have a set of facts and rules which have been entered into the database. When the interpreter is given a goal G which cannot be achieved immediately (as, for example, a goal involving **write** can), it will search the database for either

1. a fact which matches with G, or

2. a rule whose *head* matches with G.

If it finds a fact, then the goal has been achieved because it corresponds with a known fact. If it finds a rule, say

```
G :- H1 , H2 , H3 .
```

then the interpreter will try to achieve H1, H2 and H3 in turn as *subgoals*, by applying this same procedure. If, eventually, (possibly after generating further subgoals), the subgoals H1, H2 and H3 are all achieved, then the original goal G is achieved.

The process of matching goals with facts or with the heads of rules is rather easier to grasp intuitively than to describe formally. A formal description is given in Chapter 11, but for now it is best to consider illustrations. In Chapter 1 we saw how a goal

```
?- old(X).
```

was achieved because the database contained the fact

```
old(john).
```

The goal and the fact match (even though they are not identical), because the interpreter can give the value john to the variable X. We also saw the goal

```
?- wiser(jane,bill).
```

which was achieved by first matching with the head of the rule

```
wiser(X,Y) :- old(X), young(Y).
```

The matching works because the variables X and Y are available to be *instantiated*, i.e. to be given values, in this case jane and bill. As a result of this instantiation, the body of the rule becomes

```
old(jane), young(bill)
```

and so the interpreter treats separately (in turn) the subgoals

```
?- old(jane).
?- young(bill).
```

These both match (indeed are identical with) facts in the database, so the original goal is achieved with these values of X and Y.

Next let us consider a more substantial example. This will enable us to build up a broader picture of the way in which the Prolog interpreter works. Below is a list of facts and rules concerning the predicates parent, child, daughter, and female. We shall suppose that they have been entered into the database, and that the database contains no other facts and rules. In the dicussion which follows, some sample goals are suggested. It would be useful for you actually to enter these facts and rules and to try out the suggested goals, to confirm what should happen.

```
/*      RULES     */

parent(X,Y) :- child(Y,X).

daughter(X,Y) :- child(X,Y), female(X).

/*      FACTS     */

female(mary).
female(jane).

child(mary,john).
child(jane,john).
child(bill,john).
```

The goal

```
?- child(jane,john).
```

is immediately achieved because it is recognised as a known fact.
   The goal

```
?- parent(john,bill).
```

is matched with the rule for **parent** (taking X = john and Y = bill),
giving the subgoal

```
?- child(bill,john).
```

This is again immediately achieved.
   The goal

```
?- daughter(mary,john).
```

gives rise (via the rule for **daughter**) to subgoals

```
?- child(mary,john).
```
```
?- female(mary).
```

Both of these are immediately achieved.
   The goal

```
?- daughter(mary,Z).
```

gives rise to subgoals

12

```
?- child(mary,Z).
```
```
?- female(mary).
```

The first of these matches with the fact

```
child(mary,john).
```

so Z takes the value john and the original goal is satisfied.

The goal

```
?- daughter(bill,john).
```

gives rise to subgoals

```
?- child(bill,john).
```
```
?- female(bill).
```

The first of these is immediately achieved. But the second cannot be achieved – it cannot be matched with a fact or with the head of a rule. It is important to realise that the reason for failure here is precisely this. It is easy to fall into the trap of thinking that female(bill) is clearly false because of the connotations which these words carry in our minds. We must be careful to remember that the Prolog interpreter knows only what it has been told.

Lastly, the goal

```
?- daughter(D,john).
```

gives rise to the subgoals

```
?- child(D,john).
```
```
?- female(D).
```

The first matches with the fact

```
child(mary,john).
```

so D takes the value mary. Then the second subgoal becomes

```
?- female(mary).
```

which is immediately achieved. Notice that achieving (satisfying) this goal has had the effect of *finding* a daughter of john. Notice further that the daughter it finds is the *first* one it comes across. At the end of the next chapter we shall see how we can force the interpreter to look for others as well.

3 Backtracking

So far we have explored only the basic *modus operandi* of the Prolog interpreter. In this chapter and the next we discover the two features which give Prolog its real power. These are *backtracking* and *recursion*. We start by illustrating the backtracking process by means of an example. Let us return to the final example of Chapter 2, and modify it a little. Suppose that the order of the facts in the database is different, in that `child(bill,john).` is placed before the other two `child` facts. Now give the goal

```
?- daughter(D,john).
```

in effect asking, as we did previously, for the interpreter to find a daughter of `john`. As before, subgoals are generated:

```
?- child(D,john).
?- female(D).
```

But here, because the first `child` fact is `child(bill,john).`, the first subgoal is satisfied by matching with this fact, giving `D` the value `bill`. The second subgoal is then

```
?- female(bill).
```

which cannot be achieved. Clearly the interpreter has taken a wrong turning. There is nothing special about this example which has caused this. It is a feature of the way the interpreter works that it may take such wrong turnings. But the interpreter is designed to be able to recover in these circumstances, and the mechanism by which it does this is called backtracking. Before discussing it in general terms, let us continue with the above example, to see how it works in that particular case.

The goal `?- female(bill).` fails, that is, it cannot be achieved. Whenever a subgoal fails, the backtracking process is initiated. This causes the interpreter to work backwards through the subgoals which it has already achieved, searching for one which can be achieved in a different way, by matching with a different fact or rule. When it finds one, it forgets its previous matching, takes the new way, and proceeds forwards again with the same sequence of subgoals as before. In this example, this means returning to the point where the goal

    ?- child(D,john).

was satisfied. The interpreter now *re-satisfies* this in a different way. Here it can do so, by matching with another fact, namely

    child(mary,john).

thereby giving the value **mary** to D. The previous value given to D (namely **bill**) is forgotten. From this point on, the interpreter can now proceed as before, except that the second of the subgoals is now

    ?- female(mary).

which succeeds.

Backtracking is caused by *any* and *every* failure of a subgoal. If there were several **child** facts with male children occurring before the first female one, the interpreter would choose each one in turn, each time would fail on the second subgoal, backtrack, choose the next one, and proceed until the first female one was found. Of course, if there were no female ones at all, the top-level goal itself would fail, and (in this case) there could be no more backtracking because no other ways exist to satisfy the original goal.

Here is another example. Suppose that the database contains the following facts and rules.

    /*   RULES   */

    uncle(X,Y) :- parent(Z,Y), brother(X,Z).

    parent(X,Y) :- father(X,Y).
    parent(X,Y) :- mother(X,Y).

    /*   FACTS   */

    brother(george,jane).

    father(john,bill).

    mother(jane,bill).

The goal

    ?- uncle(george,bill).

16

leads to the subgoals

```
?- parent(Z,bill).
?- brother(george,Z).
```

Now the first can be matched with the head of a rule (the first rule for parent) to give the subgoal

```
?- father(Z,bill).
```

This may be satisfied by matching with a fact, taking Z to be john. We are then left to satisfy

```
?- brother(george,john).
```

But this goal fails, so the interpreter will backtrack, and will return to the most recent choice point. The previous goal (`?- father(Z,bill).`) cannot be satisfied in a different way, so we return to the goal before that, which was

```
?- parent(Z,bill).
```

This *can* be re-satisfied in another way, by matching with the head of the other rule for parent, giving the subgoal

```
?- mother(Z,bill).
```

The interpreter now proceeds as though it had reached this point the first time round. This subgoal is satisfied by taking Z to be jane, and the remaining subgoal now is

```
?- brother(george,jane).
```

which is immediately achieved.

Whenever a failure occurs, backtracking is carried out automatically and invisibly. All that the user sees is the end result; any wrong turnings are kept unrevealed. When the interpreter is dealing with substantial programs, it may well have a considerable amount of backtracking to do. Remember that *every* failure of a subgoal causes backtracking, and alternative choices are tried until one is found which works or until there are no more choices available. Backtracking is a powerful feature of Prolog, and the programmer has to learn to make positive use of the benefits which it can provide, and to be able to avoid the difficulties and inefficiencies which can arise because of it. Only experience can bring about expertise of this kind, however. We shall return to this in Chapters 12 and 13.

17

There is one situation where the user has clear and direct control over backtracking. Recall from Chapters 1 and 2 that when a goal can be satisfied in more than one way, the interpreter will choose the first way it finds. In the case of a top-level goal, the interpreter then provides a message containing details of the values chosen for variables. As we saw, in order to obtain the ?- prompt after this it is necessary to key RETURN at this point. But instead of RETURN, the interpreter will accept a *semicolon* instead. The effect of this will be to start the backtracking process, as though the previous success was in fact a failure. The interpreter will then try to satisfy the previous goal in another way. Further semicolons may be given, to force the interpreter to find as many ways of satisfying the goal in question as the user wishes, until no more possibilities remain. Of course keying RETURN instead of the semicolon will end this process. Try this out with the examples given in Chapters 1 and 2.

4 Recursion

Recursion plays a prominent role in Prolog. In practice all substantial programs in Prolog make some use of recursion, so you will have to learn to use it. A predicate is *recursive* if it is governed by a rule whose body contains a reference to the same predicate. Here is an example.

Enter the following into the database, by the procedure given in Chapter 1.

```
write_nums(0) :- write(0).
write_nums(N) :-
        write(N), nl,
        M is N - 1,
        write_nums(M).
```

Now try giving the goal

```
?- write_nums(10).
```

Can you explain the result? The interpreter is working exactly as we have seen it described in earlier chapters. Let us consider it in detail, but to keep it manageable, take instead the goal

```
?- write_nums(2).
```

This matches with the second rule for write_nums, giving four subgoals:

```
?- write(2).
?- nl.
?- M is 2 - 1.
?- write_nums(M).
```

The first two of these have obvious effects. The third gives M the value 1, and the fourth is then

```
?- write_nums(1).
```

Now we start afresh. This matches with the second rule for write_nums, giving four subgoals.

```
?- write(1).

?- nl.

?- M is 1 - 1.

?- write_nums(M).
```

It is important to realise that the variable M which appears here is *not* the same as the M which occurred in the previous set of subgoals. Variables like these are *local* to one particular call of the parent predicate (in this case write_nums). The third of these subgoals causes this M to take the value 0, and so the fourth subgoal becomes

```
?- write_nums(0).
```

This is satisfied immediately by matching with the *first* of the two rules. (Our previous goals of this form could not be matched with the first rule.) We obtain the single subgoal:

```
?- write(0).
```

which is immediately satisfied, and the interpreter has finished its job.

As in other programming languages, recursion is a potential source of error, and it must be used with care. The most obvious problem is ensuring that a recursive process does eventually stop. It is because of this that recursive predicates characteristically have two rules (possibly more) governing them – at least one rule whose body contains a recursive call, and at least one fact or rule which has no recursive call. The idea is that the process of following up the recursive calls will always lead eventually to the non-recursive fact or rule, thus stopping the recursion.

The example above would not work if the rule

```
write_nums(0) :- write(0).
```

were placed *after* the other rule in the database. Think about why this is so. Try it on the machine and see what happens. (You may need to use your system interrupt, normally CTRL-C, to recover.)

Prolog is not designed with arithmetic computations particularly in view, so it would be misleading to use that context for introductory examples of recursion. In general, recursion is more usually applied when computing with lists (see Chapter 8), or, uniquely to the language Prolog, using the structure of the database as a basis. One of the examples in Chapter 5 illustrates this.

Recursion involves a kind of self-reference which sometimes feels uncomfortable. In itself, such self-reference is always syntactically permissible (the interpreter will accept it and act on it), so there should be no cause for apprehension when giving a recursive predicate to the interpreter. The worst that can happen is that a non-terminating computation will be started, in which case the interpreter either will recognise this, and stop itself, or will continue indefinitely until stopped by a system interrupt (CTRL-C) given by the user. Here is another example, which deliberately goes too far. Enter the following rule into the database in the usual way:

```
write_stars :- write('*'), write_stars.
```

Now give the goal

```
?- write_stars.
```

You should get a screenful of stars. If it stops, press the space bar for some more. This will continue for ever, if it is allowed to. Stop it with CTRL-C. Next try an even more 'dangerous' predicate. Enter into the database:

```
keep_going :- keep_going.
```

Now give the goal

```
?- keep_going.
```

and note what happens. When you write a recursive program which doesn't terminate properly, this is the result!

5 Programs and how to run them

A program in Prolog is merely a set of definitions of predicates, i.e. a set of Prolog facts and rules. Amongst these predicates there will be one or more *top-level* predicates, i.e. predicates to carry out the task(s) for which the program was written. Running the program will consist of trying to achieve a goal. This goal will be a call of one of the top-level predicates defined in the program. In this chapter we shall see how to load and run a program, by consideration of some examples.

Example 1

As in any language, the program will reside in a file, which we may construct and modify in the standard way, using a text editor. The program in Prolog consists of Prolog facts and rules (and possibly goals too). For our first example let us consider the following very simple task. Read in two numbers from the terminal keyboard and display on the screen the two numbers together with their sum, in some sensible format. Listed below is a program which will do this. You should copy this program exactly as it is, into a file (which you might call sum, say).

```
/* top-level predicate */
sums :-
        write_prompt, read(First), nl,
        write_prompt, read(Second), nl,
        eval_sum(First,Second,Sum),
        write_result(First,Second,Sum).

/* prompt */
write_prompt :-
        write('Enter number:    ').
```

```
/* compute */
eval_sum(X,Y,S) :-
        S is X + Y.

/* display the results */
write_result(X,Y,S) :-
        write('First number:    '), write(X), nl,
        write('Second number:   '), write(Y), nl,
        write('--------------------'), nl,
        write('Sum:             '), write(S), nl.
```

You should note the following points about this program.

1. A comment begins with /* and ends with */.

2. The top-level predicate here is **sums**. As it happens, this predicate has no arguments. It is common, but not universal, for this to be the case. Arguments in the top-level predicate are in effect parameters which could be used either to pass data in to the program or to pass results out. In this case that mechanism is not used - instead data is explicitly read and written from/to the terminal. See Example 3.

3. The subgoals in the body of the rule for **sums** will, in effect, be executed in sequence, so these can sensibly be regarded as comprising a program or algorithm. This kind of breakdown into subgoals reflects ordinary programming practice, whether it be in Prolog (with subgoals) or in another language like Pascal (with a top-level algorithm implemented via procedure calls).

4. In Prolog, all identifiers which start with an upper case letter are recognised as variables. As in other languages, it can be helpful to choose appropriate names for variables.

5. The built-in predicate **read** will read a value given by the user at the terminal. Execution by the interpreter will be suspended until input has been given. Remember to follow all input by a full stop and RETURN. For example, **read(First)**, as a goal, will succeed when a value has been given by the user, and will cause this value to be given to the variable **First**.

6. Of course, the predicate **eval_sum** is not really necessary. Instead of the occurrence of

```
eval_sum(First,Second,Sum)
```

in the body of the rule for **sums**, we could have just

```
Sum is First + Second.
```

But this example is illustrative of a way of proceeding, and in general the details of computations should not appear at the top level of our program unless it is very simple. Again, this is a feature of programming in any language. Indeed Prolog makes this kind of breakdown of a task really quite convenient.

7. Formatting can improve readability. In Prolog code we may insert spaces, tabs, blank lines and comments anywhere without affecting the sense. If used sensibly this can make even complicated programs readable.

8. In the above program, the order in which the rules appear is unimportant. The rule for **sums** could come after the others. But it makes programs easier to read if, as far as possible, the place where a predicate is called precedes the place where it is defined, and the top-level predicate(s) appear first. But remember that (as we saw in Chapter 4) there are some circumstances where it is essential that the facts and rules come in a particular order.

9. It may be necessary to include an extra blank line at the end of the file. This is a quirk of some systems. Without it, the last fact or rule in the file may not be loaded properly.

Now how do we run this program? Enter the Prolog system as usual and load the program by giving the goal ?- [sum]. The goal consists of the name of the file enclosed in square brackets. (We have chosen a particularly simple name for the file containing our program. A file name may contain non-alphanumeric characters, typically full stops, slashes or square brackets. In such cases when we load a program from a file, the file name must be enclosed in single quotes, e.g. ?- ['sums.pro'].) Giving this form of goal will cause the program to be transferred from the file into the database, unless there are errors in the program, in which case this goal will fail, giving some indication of the nature and location of the error (not always very helpful). If there is an error, leave Prolog, edit the file, re-enter Prolog and try again. Once the program has been transferred into the database, the predicates defined in the file **sum** are available. So to run the program, give the goal

```
?- sums.
```

The next thing which appears on the screen will be the prompt

```
Enter number:
```

and you should key in a number, say 387 (followed by a full stop and RETURN). The screen will then show another prompt, and you should key in another number similarly, say 544. The screen will now show

```
First number:    387
Second number:   544
--------------------
Sum:             931
```

And then, because the goal ?- sums has been satisfied, the usual message is then displayed to indicate this. After another RETURN, the ?- prompt reappears.

Exercise

Modify the above program so that it will compute and output also the product of the two numbers in an appropriate format.

The program above exemplifies a simple form: input, compute, output. This form can be found in more complicated Prolog programs. Notice that this form in itself does not involve any backtracking or recursion, although of course the individual parts may do.

Example 2

Here Prolog is used for a different sort of task. Below is another program, which may be stored, say, in a file called exam.

```
/* top-level predicate */
passlist :-
        passed(Student),
        write(Student), nl,
        fail.
passlist.

/* find name and mark, and test whether a pass */
passed(Student) :-
        mark(Student,X),
        X > 49.

/* Now the list of names and marks */
```

```
mark(brown,61).
mark(cook,87).
mark(frame,43).
mark(lucas,55).
mark(nelson,69).
mark(page,74).
mark(stewart,26).
mark(webster,66).
mark(white,52).
```

To load this program, follow the procedure given for the first example above, giving the goal ?- [exam].

To run the program, give the top-level predicate as a goal:

```
?- passlist.
```

The effect will be to have the names

```
brown
cook
lucas
nelson
page
webster
white
```

listed on the screen. This is by no means as straightforward as the previous example, so let us examine how this happens. The body of the rule for passlist ends with fail. This is a built-in predicate which, as its name suggests, always fails. Its sole purpose is as a means for the programmer to ensure that backtracking takes place. In this program, positive use of backtracking is being made, and its effect is to carry out a search. Specifically, to satisfy the goal ?- passlist. the interpreter must first satisfy the subgoal ?- passed(Student). To do this it uses the rule for passed, requiring that the subgoal ?- mark(Student,X). be satisfied. This is done by matching with the first fact for mark, giving the value brown to the variable Student and the value 61 to the variable X. The subgoal ?- X > 49. now becomes ?- 61 > 49. which succeeds immediately, thus ensuring that the goal ?- passed(Student). has been satisfied, with Student being given the value brown. The next subgoal causes the name brown to be written, and after the nl, we reach the subgoal ?- fail. Backtracking occurs. The interpreter returns to the earlier subgoals, trying to find one which can be re-satisfied in a different way. Now nl cannot be re-satisfied (this is the way it happens to be designed), and similarly no goal

27

involving **read** or **write** can be re-satisfied. So the interpreter returns to **?-passed(Student)**. In the same way as before, this is satisfied with **Student** being given the value **cook**, which is just the next one to be found. Again, the name is displayed and the **fail** causes backtracking. This time in trying to re-satisfy **?- passed(Student)**. the name **frame** is found, but the corresponding mark is **43**, so the goal **?- 43 > 49**. fails, causing backtracking. This time the interpreter needs to backtrack only as far as the subgoal **?- mark(Student,X)**. The name **frame** has been considered, rejected and forgotten, and the next name, **lucas**, is considered in the same way. And so on. Eventually, all of the **mark** facts will have been considered, and at that stage, **?- passed(Student)**. cannot be further re-satisfied. One more backtrack takes place. The interpreter tries to re-satisfy **?- passlist**. in a different way. And it can, by using the fact **passlist**. This succeeds immediately, and the computation ends.

This sort of program extracts information from a store. In this case the store (the facts concerning the predicate **mark**) is integrated into the program, which is not a likely situation in practice. It served to provide us with an example of Prolog in action. But the example can be easily modified to make it more like the real thing. We may store the data in one file and the extraction program in another. The **mark** facts could be placed in a file called **marks.dat**, say, and the rest of the above program placed in the file **exam.pro**. Before running the program we would now have to load both files, by

```
?- ['marks.dat','exam.pro'].
```

Of course, any other file of **mark** facts could be used with the same **exam** program, as long as the format of the facts was the same.

Exercise

Modify the above program so that the mark obtained by each passing student is displayed alongside the name.

Example 3

Here is a recursive program, where the recursion uses the structure of the database, as mentioned in Chapter 4. Construct a file containing the following program, and load it as described in the earlier examples.

```
/* definition of 'royal' */
royal(george6).
```

```
royal(X) :-
        parent(Y,X),
        royal(Y).

/* facts about 'parent' */
parent(george6,elizabeth).
parent(george6,margaret).
parent(philip,charles).
parent(elizabeth,charles).
parent(charles,william).
parent(diana,william).
```

The predicate **royal** is recursive. Try the following goals:

```
?- royal(george6).
?- royal(philip).
?- royal(william).
?- royal(margaret).
?- royal(diana).
```

Work out the steps which the interpreter takes in each case. Notice that there is some backtracking involved in the third one, because of a wrong choice which the interpreter makes during the process. Be sure you understand why the second and last ones fail. The recursion process works back through the family tree (represented by the 'parent' facts). If it reaches **george6** then it succeeds. Otherwise it fails.

Exercise

Assuming the existence of a database of facts about the predicate **parent**, like the one above, but possibly more extensive, and not necessarily limited to the royal family, give a recursive definition (a fact and a rule) of a predicate **forebear**, such that **forebear(X,Y)** is to mean "X is an ancestor of Y".

Example 4

The final example of the chapter is to emphasise a common form of predicate, which might be described as the 'functional' form. The predicate **eval_sum**, given in the first example above, is one of these. It has three arguments, two of which in effect carry input values, the other standing for an output value. Satisfying the predicate has the effect of computing a function value and then giving this value to the output variable (by means of Prolog's instantiation process). This may seem an odd way to work, but it is in direct analogy with the way in which a procedure in Pascal or Modula-2 may be used to calculate values of a function, using a variable parameter for the output. The only difference is that in Prolog there is no formal way to identify those arguments in a predicate which are to stand for variable parameters. It helps to include comments in Prolog code which give this kind of information.

Here is another example of a functional predicate.

```
/* to compute the larger of two numbers,
       here represented by X and Y */
max(X,Y,Y) :- X < Y.
max(X,Y,X) :- X >= Y.
```

The third argument gives the output. If the second argument has the larger value, the the first rule will succeed, and the third argument will be instantiated to the value of Y. Otherwise the first rule will fail, and backtracking will cause the second rule to be used. This will then succeed, and the third argument will be instantiated to the value of X.

For example, the goal

```
?- max(3,5,Z).
```

will succeed with Z = 5 because the goal matches the head of the first rule, with X = 3, Y = 5, and Z = 5, and the subgoal ?- 3 < 5. then succeeds.

Also, the goal

```
?- max(4,2,Z).
```

succeeds with Z = 4 because (after matching with the first rule has led to the subgoal ?- 4 < 2. which fails), matching with the second rule, with X = 4, Y = 2, Z = 4 succeeds.

It could be argued that this Prolog version of max is inefficient, because the second rule contains a test which is unnecessary — the second rule will ever be applied only after the first rule has failed, i.e. after the subgoal ?- X < Y. has failed. For the moment, we should accept such inefficiencies (indeed there is a positive benefit in readability gained by the inclusion of the redundant test). Later (in Chapter 13) we shall see a way of removing this and similar inefficiencies, using the 'cut', but at some cost in readability.

Exercise

Write a program which will compute in a similar way the largest
of three given integers.

6 Programs and how to write them

Specification

Prolog may appear to be different from other programming languages. But the kind of thought required in the process of writing a program is very similar. And the nature of Prolog is such that *less* thought may be required. The purpose of this chapter is to show what this means in practice and to show just how the nature of Prolog facilitates program construction.

Forget for a moment about the Prolog interpreter, and think about a Prolog rule:

```
uncle(X,Y) :- brother(X,Z), parent(Z,Y).
```

The :- symbol means 'if', and the comma means 'and'. So this can be read as

X is an uncle of Y if X is a brother of (some) Z and Z is a parent of Y.

This in turn is a true statement about the relationships involved. Indeed it could be (at least part of) a definition of the term 'uncle'. This is a general feature of Prolog rules. The part to the right of the :- gives a description of circumstances in which the part to the left of the :- is true.

This particular example may not on the face of it be helpful in relating Prolog to ordinary programming tasks. It seems to deal just with relationships between objects and not with operations or transformations on objects. But now think not of programming, but of *specification*. Think not of 'how', but rather think of 'what'. The customary idea of specification of a task is an expression of a relationship between input and output. Here are some examples:

1. The value of B is twice the value of A.

2. M is the maternal grandmother of P.

3. Student S obtained a pass in course C.

4. £P invested at X% interest per annum compound will amount to £A after N years.

These all express relationships (they are examples of predicates). They are all specifications, although in some cases there is ambiguity over what is to be input and what is to be output. For example, 1. may specify either multiplication by 2 or division by 2. Taking each in turn, then, we may take these as specifications for the following tasks.

1. Multiplication by 2.

2. Find the name of the maternal grandmother of a given person.

3. Find whether a given student obtained a pass in a given course.

4. Find the value after a given number of years of a given initial investment, where interest is compounded at a given rate per annum.

Refining a Specification

Relationships can express specifications. Conventionally, a programmer has to convert a specification (usually informal and often unwritten) into a sequence of instructions. These instructions embody the detail of 'how' the requisite values are to be computed, while ensuring that they have the stipulated relationship with the input. The first stage of this process might be an analysis of the specification, to see whether the task can be broken down into smaller tasks. And indeed this might be iterated. But at some stage there is a leap from specification to program, from description to instructions, from 'what' to 'how'. In Prolog, however, this leap is (in theory at least) absent. Prolog *programs* have the descriptive (*declarative*) nature which is a property of specifications. Indeed Prolog programs can be regarded as specifications. And programming in Prolog is a process of refining a specification, the objective of the refinement being to express it in terms which are known to the interpreter, either through being built-in (as arithmetic operations are) or through being currently held in the database. Let us reconsider the four examples above.

1.   double(A,B) :- B is A * 2.

It could sensibly be said that there is no *program* here. We have merely couched the specification in terms which are amenable to the Prolog interpreter. Note the use of is to evaluate an arithmetic expression. More detail about arithmetic is given in Chapter 9.

2. To refine this specification usefully, we need to know what form of records are kept, and we need to know what constitutes a pass. So one refinement might be:

```
passed(S,C) :-
        coursemark(C,S,M),
        M > 49.
```

This refinement will be sensible if we have a database of `coursemark` facts, with numerical marks, and that the pass mark is 50.

Alternatively:

```
passed(S,C) :-
        coursegrade(C,S,a);
        coursegrade(C,S,b);
        coursegrade(C,S,c).
```

is a refinement based on different assumptions.

3.
```
        m_grandmother(M,P) :-
                mother(M,Z),
                mother(Z,P).
```

will be a useful refinement of this specification if our database contains facts about the predicate `mother`.

4. This we might treat in one of two ways. There is a mathematical formula which gives the required value. It is:

$$A = P * (1 + X/100)^N.$$

So we might regard this formula as providing a refinement of the specification:

```
amount(P,X,N,A) :-
        A is P * (1 + X/100)^N.
```

Alternatively, we might be unaware of this formula, and we might seek to refine the specification for ourselves, thus:

£P invested at X% per annum will amount to £P1 after one year, and £P1 invested at X% per annum will amount to £A after N - 1 further years.

In Prolog we might write this:

```
amount(P,X,N,A) :-
        one_year(P,X,P1),
        M is N - 1,
        amount(P1,X,M,A).
```

Before we refine **one_year**, notice that this version of **amount** is recursive, and it is not yet quite right. What is wrong is that the recursive call of **amount** does not say exactly what we need, and consequently a run of this program will never terminate. Explicitly, the **N - 1** further years might in fact be *no* years, and this case has not been covered. We can make it right by extending the definition of **amount** by including the fact

```
amount(P,X,0,P).
```

For operational reasons (because of the way the Prolog interpreter works) this fact will have to be inserted before the rule. This aspect of recursion was mentioned in Chapter 4.

All that remains is to refine **one_year**:

```
one_year(P,X,P1) :-
        P1 is P + (P*X/100).
```

The refinement of a specification may involve combinations of subspecifications either as alternatives (semicolon) or as conjunctions (comma). Moreover, it can proceed in stages. After a breakdown into subspecifications, any of the subspecifications can itself be further broken down, and so on. This will introduce (in Prolog) intermediate predicates, instances of which will be treated by the interpreter as subgoals.

The point is that Prolog is declarative, as a specification is, and programs in Prolog are not sequences of instructions (so the word 'program' is really a misnomer). In a sense, when writing a program in Prolog, the problem and the solution are different ways of expressing the same thing. What guides us in programming is knowledge of what we have to work with (the contents of the database, the built-in facilities of Prolog, and the form of any user input). And of course we do have to be aware of the way in which the Prolog interpreter operates, as described elsewhere in this book.

Let us end the chapter with two further examples.

Example

Suppose that the database contains facts for predicates `father`, `mother`, `birth` and `death`. The last two are to give years of birth and death for named people. Consider the following specification:

> The age at death (in years) of the maternal grandmother of person P was A.

First refinement:

> The maternal grandmother of P was M, and the age at death of M was A years.

In Prolog:

```
m_g_age(P,A) :-
        m_grandmother(M,P),
        age_at_death(M,A).
```

Second refinement (`m_grandmother`):

```
m_grandmother(M,P) :-
        mother(M,Z),
        mother(Z,P).
```

Second refinement (`age_at_death`):

```
age_at_death(M,A) :-
        birth(M,Birthdate),
        death(M,Deathdate),
        A is Deathdate - Birthdate.
```

Of course, if the birthdate and death date are in years only, then the age reckoned above might in fact be incorrect. Representation of exact dates involves more complex structures, so this example has been simplified. We shall see in Chapter 7 how structured data can be represented. Notice also that we have made the simplifying assumption that the appropriate birth and death records are in the database.

Exercise

A person will have two grandmothers, of course. Refine the following specification into Prolog code:

> G is the name of the grandmother of P who lived the longer (assuming that both are dead).

Example

Suppose that we have a database of facts about exchange rates at three financial centres, in the form

```
exchange(pound,dollar,london,1.8235).
exchange(dollar,yen,new_york,126.05).
exchange(pound,dmark,tokyo,3.1399).
```

Consider the following specification:

> The best rate of exchange available from currency C1 to currency C2 is R.

This predicate may be represented in Prolog as best_rate(C1,C2,R). A first refinement might then be expressed by the Prolog rule:

```
best_rate(C1,C2,R) :-
        rate(C1,C2,london,R1),
        rate(C1,C2,new_york,R2),
        rate(C1,C2,tokyo,R3),
        max3(R1,R2,R3,R).
```

The intended meaning of max3 should be clear, and we can further refine this as follows:

```
max3(A1,A2,A3,A) :-
        max(A1,A2,T),
        max(A3,T,A).
```

Further, the intended meaning of max should be clear, and we can go to a third level of refinement:

```
max(A,B,B) :- A < B.
max(A,B,A) :- A >= B.
```

This, of course, is the same predicate max which was discussed in Chapter 5. Now returning to the first refinement, you will have noticed that the predicate rate is used, rather than exchange. This is purely because of the form of the stored information. We may suppose that only one rate is given for each pair of currencies at each place, and that the rate for trading in the opposite direction is the inverse of the rate given. We therefore need the refinement

```
rate(C1,C2,P,R) :-
        exchange(C1,C2,P,R);
        (exchange(C2,C1,P,S), R is 1/S).
```

Our Prolog program is now complete. It consists of the rule for the top-level predicate `best_rate`, together with the rules for the intermediate predicates `rate`, `max3` and `max`.

Here is another specification:

> Converting currency C1 into currency C2, thence into currency C3 (different from C1), and then back into currency C1, all at the best available rates, will result in a proportional gain or loss of Q.

In Prolog (using `best_rate` from above):

```
triple_rate(C1,C2,C3,Q) :-
        best_rate(C1,C2,R1),
        best_rate(C2,C3,R2), not(C3 = C1),
        best_rate(C3,C1,R3),
        Q is R1 * R2 * R3.
```

Notice that we have carried the requirement that C3 be different from C1 explicitly into the code. In fact, it is unnecessary to do so, because the subspecification `best_rate(C3,C1,R3)` will be impossible to satisfy if C3 is the same as C1.

And here is a final specification:

> It is possible to make a significant proportional profit Q, starting with currency C, selling successively into two other currencies and back to C.

We can obviously use `triple_rate` in refining this one. But we need to quantify the meaning of 'significant' before we can write down a Prolog rule. Let us say that a gain is significant if it is greater than 2%. Then

```
sig_profit(C,Q) :-
        triple_rate(C,C2,C3,Q),
        Q > 1.02.
```

This code is still declarative. The body of the rule gives circumstances in which a significant profit can be made. We may regard C as input, Q as output, and C2 and C3 are variables which must have values, but whose actual values are not passed out. The Prolog interpreter would use a process of trial and error (backtracking) to find values for C2 and C3.

The above example has clearly been simplified in order to help illustrate the points at issue. When dealing with a real situation of this kind, it is likely that other information will be sought, for example the places where the best rates can be obtained, or the various combinations of places where the best composite deals can be made. As an exercise, consider these questions.

Exercises

Refine the following specifications into Prolog code.

R is the best rate of exchange from currency C1 into currency C2, and it is obtainable in place P.

Starting with currency C1, selling into currency C2 at place P1, and thence into currency C3 at place P2, and back into currency C1 at place P3 will yield a proportional gain or loss of Q. (Here we are not necessarily concerned with the *best* rates.)

7   Data Structures

There are only two ways to build structured data objects in Prolog – as *structures* or as *lists*. Strictly a list is a certain kind of Prolog structure, but lists are particularly important and they are used in distinctive ways, so it is best to consider them separately, as we shall in the next chapter.

A structure is just a predicate with arguments, of the kind we have already seen. (In Chapter 2 we used the term 'single expressions'.) Here are some structures:

```
mark(cook,87)
royal(george6)
father(john,bill)
```

We have been accustomed to thinking of these as assertions. But it is also possible to regard structures merely as records where information is stored. For example

```
king('England','Henry',8,1509,1547)
```

is a structure which begins to look like an entry in a database of historical information. A more complex example might be

```
book('Structured Computer Organization',
     'Tanenbaum',
     'Prentice-Hall',
     1976)
```

The arguments in this structure contain details about a book. Corresponding details for other books could be held in structures with a similar form. The single quotes in both the above examples are necessary. The reasons for this will be covered in Chapter 10.

Given a Prolog database consisting of **book** facts like the above, it is exceedingly easy to extract information. For example

```
yearlist76 :-
        book(Title,Author,Publisher,1976),
```

41

```
        write(Title), nl,
        fail.
    yearlist76.
```

This is a short program which defines the predicate **yearlist76**. Giving the goal **?- yearlist76.** will cause all titles of books known to the database and published in the year 1976 to be written out. Note that backtracking causes looping in this example, as in one of the examples given in Chapter 5. As it stands, however, this is not very practical – it would be much better to allow a year to be specified by the user in the top-level goal. This is still very simple:

```
    yearlist(Date) :-
        book(Title,Author,Publisher,Date),
        write(Title), nl,
        fail.
    yearlist(Date).
```

Here the variable **Date** carries information *in* to the call of **yearlist**, whereas the other variables which occur are entirely *local*. Indeed the only other variable which serves a useful purpose is **Title**. The others (**Author** and **Publisher**) are certainly given values each time that **book(Title,Author,Publisher,Date)** is matched with a known structure, but these values are never used. Prolog has a convenient way of dealing with such situations – the *anonymous* variable. The above definition could have been written as:

```
    yearlist(Date) :-
        book(Title,_,_,Date),
        write(Title), nl,
        fail.
    yearlist(Date).
```

The underscore is the anonymous variable. It matches with *anything*, but does not hold a value. So it is used for matching structures when there are some parts of the structures whose values we do not care about, and do not need to know.

As an exercise, try to write other predicates which will extract other information from such a **book** database. For example, list the titles and dates of all known books from a given publisher. As a slightly harder exercise, list the authors of all known books published *after* a given date. As a further exercise, make these into 'user-friendly' programs which give appropriate prompts and provide appropriate messages in cases where no information is found.

The **book** structure used as an example here is quite a simple one. Prolog structures can be much more complex, and can be nested. For example, a database of genealogical information might consist of 'event' records, held as facts of the following forms.

```
event( date(7,'March',1958),
       birth('John Smith',
             male,
             parents('James Smith','Mary Jones')) ).

event( date(22,'August',1955),
       marriage('James Smith','Mary Jones') ).

event( date(13,'May',1970),
       death('George Smith') ).
```

The way that names are represented here is not very useful. We shall be able to do it better when we know how to use lists. (The most obvious problem is in identifying the parts of a name, for example the surname.) Lists will likewise be useful in making the **book** structure more flexible, for example in coping with books which have more than one author. We shall return to these examples.

Notice that when structures are used in this way as records, each occurrence of the structure must have the same number of arguments. The **event** facts may record various kinds of event, but the structure must must be consistent in order to be useful. But of course the individual components which occur in the structure may have different forms, as **birth, marriage** and **death** have in the example.

8 Lists

Lists play a pervasive role in Prolog. They provide the normal way of combining various data items into a single structure, particularly when the number of items is either unknown or subject to variation. At its simplest, a list is represented in Prolog like this:

```
[4,7,9,3,6]
[john,smith]
```

The items are separated by commas and the whole is enclosed by square brackets. The items in a list need not be distinct:

```
[4,7,4,9,3,6,7]
```

is a list with seven members which is certainly different from the first one above. Also the items in a list need not be related in any way, and need not even be of the same kind:

```
[john,smith,33,'Ford Sierra']
```

is an acceptable list. Furthermore, the items in a list may themselves be lists:

```
[smith,[7,10,14]]
```

might be a sensible list.

It is necessary to have a notation for a list with no members.

[] denotes the empty list.

It is essential to bear in mind the distinction between a list with a single member and the object which is that single member.

[smith] is a list with a single member.

smith is that single member.

[7] is a list with a single member.

7 is that single member.

What we have so far is helpful as an intuitive guide to the structure of lists. We have not yet seen how Prolog can operate on and make use of lists. Almost always, this involves recursion. A very simple illustration is a predicate which will cause the members of a list to be written out in sequence. In words, here is how Prolog can do this.

1. If the list is empty, do nothing.

2. Otherwise, write the first member of the list, then

3. recursively write out the rest of the list, using this process.

To do this, Prolog has to have a way of extracting the first member (the *head*) and the rest (the *tail*) of a non-empty list. This brings us to another way in which lists may be represented:

    [H|T]

denotes the list whose head is H and whose tail is T. Using this notation we can see how to write out the members of a list:

```
writeout([]).

writeout([H|T]) :-
        write(H),
        nl,
        writeout(T).
```

This predicate is recursive. Indeed it is formally very similar to the first example of a recursive predicate given in Chapter 4. It writes the members of any list, each on a separate line. Be sure that you understand the purpose of the fact writeout([]).

This example also illustrates another feature of Prolog's matching process. The head of the rule above is

    writeout([H|T]).

When (say) the goal

    ?- writeout([smith,jones,robinson]).

is given, the interpreter will try to match this with a fact or with the head of a rule. It cannot match with writeout([]), but it can match with writeout([H|T]), by giving H the value smith and giving T the value [jones,robinson]. Previously the head of a rule has usually had arguments which were themselves variables. Here the head of the rule has an argument which is a more complex object, namely [H|T]. But the matching process can cope with this just as well. Details of this are given in Chapter 11.

It may be instructive to follow this example through. The first stage yields the subgoals

```
?- write(smith).

?- nl.

?- writeout([jones,robinson]).
```

To achieve the last of these, we match with the rule again, this time with H = jones and T = [robinson], giving the subgoals

```
?- write(jones).

?- nl.

?- writeout([robinson]).
```

Now to achieve the last of these, we match with the rule again, with H = robinson and T = []. (Take the head away from a list with only one member, and the rest is the empty list.) The rule yields the subgoals

```
?- write(robinson).

?- nl.

?- writeout([]).
```

The last of these matches with the fact, and is immediately achieved.

A common requirement is to search a list, i.e. to find whether a given object is a member of a given list. A simple recursion will do this.

```
member(X,[X|_]).

member(X,[_|T]) :- member(X,T).
```

Notice the use of the anonymous variable (the underscore) in this example. You should convince yourself that member serves the required purpose, if necessary by following through (by hand) some simple cases, such as the goals

```
?- member(1,[1,2,3]).

?- member(1,[3,2,1]).

?- member(4,[1,2,3]).
```

Data structures as discussed in Chapter 7 suffer from a certain rigidity. All occurrences of a predicate must have the same number of arguments. For example, the book record structure allowed one argument for the author's name. If there is more than one author, a convenient representation would be to have in this position in the structure a list of authors' names. To be uniform, of course, we would have to have a list even in cases where there was only one author. For example:

```
book('Programming in Prolog',
     ['Clocksin','Mellish'],
     'Springer-Verlag',
     1981)

book('Structured Computer Organization',
     ['Tanenbaum'],
     'Prentice-Hall',
     1976)
```

Likewise, if we wish to record people's full names, including surname and forenames, we might use a list structure, e.g.

```
[smith,john,frederick]
```

This will conveniently allow us to represent names by a single structure, irrespective of the number of forenames. Of course, if we wish to use upper case letters in names, single quotes must be inserted. For example, a book record might be

```
book('Programming in Prolog',
     [['Clocksin','William'],['Mellish','Christopher']],
     'Springer-Verlag',
     1981)
```

Here are some predicates which operate on lists.

1.   double([],[]).

            double([H|T],[K|U]) :- K is 2 * H, double(T,U).

The effect of the goal

```
?- double([1,2,3],L).
```

is to give L the value [2,4,6]. This is an example of a predicate which has in input argument (the first) and an output argument (the second) and in operation it actually computes a function value.

2.   `alt([],[]).`

          `alt([X],[X]).`

          `alt([A,B|T],[A|U]) :- alt(T,U).`

This is another 'functional' predicate. An example of its use is:

    `?- alt([1,2,3,4,5,6],L).`

This will succeed with L = [1,3,5]. Notice that for this recursive predicate we need *two* 'base cases' – two facts which stop the recursion.

3.   `append([],L,L).`

          `append([A|L1],L2,[A|L3]) :- append(L1,L2,L3).`

This one is tricky, but important, so you should make an effort to understand it. Its effect is to concatenate two lists (the first two arguments), to give the result in the third argument. For example

    `?- append([1,2],[7,8,9],L).`

will succeed, with L = [1,2,7,8,9]. You should follow through this example by hand, to make sure that you understand how the interpreter treats it.

4.   `reverse([],[]).`

          `reverse([H|T],L) :-`
                `reverse(T,U),`
                `append(U,[H],L).`

Work this one out for yourself!

9 Arithmetic

Prolog was not originally designed with arithmetic computations in mind. Indeed early versions of Prolog did not support floating point numbers or even negative integers. On some systems the limit on the size of numbers was impractically low. This book is not about the use of Prolog for complex applications involving numerical computations, so this chapter will be limited to merely describing the basic facilities which Prolog provides, and the ways in which they can be used. We start with *integers*, which on some systems might mean merely positive integers.

The operators which may be used to construct *arithmetic expressions* are

+	addition
*	multiplication
–	subtraction
/	integer division
mod	remainder
–	unary minus (some systems do not have this)

Notes:

- Remember that arithmetic expressions are not numbers. The value of an arithmetic expression may be obtained by means of the predicate **is**.

- On a system without negative numbers, there is no unary minus operator. On such systems, care is required with subtraction – for example **2 – 3** will have a value (computed via **is**), although that value will not be **–1**. It will depend on the way the system is set up, and may well be **16383**.

- On a system with negative numbers, the unary minus operator may be denoted by a different symbol, possibly ˜.

- An illustration. The goal

```
?- X is (13 - (41/6)) * (4 + 1).
```

gives X the value 35.

Recent Prolog systems now have fully practical arithmetic, very much like other computer languages. Generally, integer and real (floating-point) values can be mixed in an expression – there is no rigid separation of the two types. Real numbers have two representations:

0.367E+2 is the same number as 36.7

-4.215E-4 is the same number as -0.00004215

Here is a list of operators available in a system with floating-point arithmetic:

+	addition
*	multiplication
-	subtraction
/	division (not integer division)
^	raise to a power
-	unary minus
sqrt	square root
exp	exponential (*e* to a power)
log	logarithm (base *e*)
log10	logarithm (base 10)
sin	natural sine
cos	natural cosine
tan	natural tangent
asin	arc sine
acos	arc cosine
atan	arc tangent

In addition, the integer operations

//	integer division
mod	remainder

may be available, restricted to operate on integers.

Unfortunately, there are variations in the notations used for the operations in the above list. You should consult the manual for your own system if there is any doubt about the symbols which it uses.

Numerical values can be *compared*. The following are built-in, and may be used in the obvious way to test values. The only point to note is that only variables or specific numbers may occur in comparisons. More complex expressions must be evaluated before they can be compared. And at the time of the comparison, any variables concerned must have values.

<	is less than
>	is greater than
=<	is equal to or less than
>=	is greater than or equal to

Of course, Prolog can test for equality of values also. But equality is a broader question, because expressions of any kind can be tested for equality. Discussion of this is left until Chapter 11. But here we should note that besides =, there is also =:=. This provides a test of whether two given arithmetic expressions have the same *value*. For example, the goal

```
?- 3 + 2 = 4 + 1.
```

will fail, because 3 + 2 and 4 + 1 are *different* expressions. But the goal

```
?- 3 + 2 =:= 4 + 1.
```

will succeed, because the interpreter will first evaluate the two expressions, and then test for equality.

To end the chapter, here are two example programs.

Example

Here is a program which computes the average of a given list of numbers.

```
/* Top-level predicate */
average(L,X) :-
        sum(L,S),
        length(L,N),
        X is S/N.

/* Now the subsidiary predicate */
sum([],0).
```

```
sum([H|T],P) :-
        sum(T,Z),
        P is Z + H.

/* The predicate 'length' is a built-in
   predicate.  Given a list in its first
   argument, it returns the length of that
   list in its second argument. */
```

Try out this program according to the procedure described in Chapter 5. Give some goals like

```
?- average([2,4,6,8],X).
```

Note that the subsidiary predicate sum can be easily tested by trying goals such as

```
?- sum([2,4,6,8],S).
```

Example

The above program is simple and easy to follow because its structure indicates the way in which it works. So here is a challenge! Below is another program which computes the average of a given list of numbers. See if you can follow how it works.

```
/* Top-level predicate */
average(L,X) :- av(L,0,0,X).

/* Subsidiary predicate */
av([],S,N,X) :- X is S/N.

av([H|T],S,N,X) :-
        SS is S + H,
        NN is N + 1,
        av(T,SS,NN,X).
```

This second program is not particularly recommended, because readability is one prime requirement for programs, and the first one wins easily on that score. But the second has the virtue that the computations of the length and the sum are integrated into one recursion. In the first version, these two computations are completely separate, even though they involve the same list and both can be carried out by the same kind of recursive process. The second version illustrates a standard way of working in more

advanced Prolog programming – the use of additional arguments (such as
the S and N above) whose purpose is to hold intermediate values during a
computation. Here these stand for the 'sum so far' and the 'length so far'
respectively.

10 Formalities

Details about syntax have been deliberately avoided up till now. There are two reasons for this. First, it is not necessary to know all of the formal rules of the game before being able to take part, and indeed taking part provides a stimulus towards learning the rules. And second, the aim of this book is not to be an abstract description of the language – it is to show how to use the language. However, it is necessary to understand some at least of the formal details in order to be able to use it properly, and we cannot postpone this any longer.

Terms

Legal expressions in Prolog are called 'terms'. Goals are terms, facts and rules are terms, and the meaningful constituent parts of such terms are terms also. Formally:

Every Prolog *term* is one of the following

- a constant

- a variable

- a structure

Now we must describe what these are. Every *constant* is one of the following

- a number

- an atom

Numbers have been discussed in Chapter 9.

An *atom* is made up of characters according to one of the following descriptions.

1. Consisting entirely of alphanumeric characters together with the underscore, and starting with a lower-case letter.

2. Consisting of any characters whatever, but enclosed in single quotes. If it is desired to include a single quote in such an atom, it must be repeated, e.g. `'Bill''s house'` is an atom.

3. Being one of a number of special (built-in, known to the interpreter) combinations of non-alphanumeric characters. Examples are `?-`, `:-`, `==`, `[]`, `=<`. There are several more of these, and we shall encounter most of them as we proceed. Most, but not all, are operators – see below and see Chapter 19.

It is important to realise that an atom is a constant, i.e. a value, just as a number is a value. An atom is not an identifier in the usual sense of that word.

Next, a *variable* is composed of alphanumeric characters and underscores, but starting with an upper-case letter or an underscore. An underscore on its own is a special (anonymous) variable. A variable may be thought of as an identifier, but it does not behave in the same way as variables in other languages.

Last, a *structure* has two parts, a *functor*, which must be an atom, and, enclosed in parentheses, one or more *arguments*, which may be terms of any kind, separated by commas.

Examples

```
father(john, bill)
ATOM  ATOM  ATOM

father(  X   ,  bill)
ATOM  VARIABLE   ATOM

father( Father ,   Son)
ATOM  VARIABLE  VARIABLE
```

Operators

Every legal expression in Prolog which is not a constant or a variable is a structure, and has a functor and arguments. You should remember this. In order to make sense of it, we have to recognise that there are different ways to represent (on paper or on the screen) structures of certain kinds. Some particular atoms are known to the interpreter to be be 'operators' (details are given in Chapter 19). A structure whose functor is an operator may have alternative forms, either prefix (standard) or infix (the non-standard form in Prolog). For example, + is an operator in Prolog. As we noted earlier, 2 + 3 is an expression (a structure) not a number. Indeed

```
2 + 3    and    +(2,3)
```

are two ways to represent the same Prolog structure.
Another operator is =.

```
X = Y    and    =(X,Y)
```

are representations of the same structure. Further, :- is an operator, so facts and rules are structures.

Facts and Rules

First consider an example. The rule

```
wiser(X,Y) :- old(X), young(Y).
```

is a Prolog structure which may be written

```
':-'(wiser(X,Y),(old(X),young(Y)))
```

Note that the functor ':-' has two arguments always – the head and body of the rule. (See the end of this chapter for a discussion about quotation marks.) The body of this rule is a structure also, of course. It is old(X),young(Y). The functor in this structure is, confusingly, the comma. This comma means 'and', and is an operator. So old(X),young(Y), when written out in full, is

```
','(old(X),young(Y))
```

The comma is a *binary* operator. When a rule body contains more than two subgoals, the interpreter will interpret them thus:

```
g1,g2,g3,g4    means    g1,(g2,(g3,g4)))
```

The semicolon (meaning 'or') is also an operator, and is treated in a similar way by the interpreter.
Next we consider facts in a similar way. On the face of it a fact looks just like a structure. For example

```
old(john).
```

is a fact. But it must be distinguished from the structure

```
old(john)
```

A structure becomes a fact when it is 'asserted' into the database, and only then. Actually, a fact is a special kind of rule. For example

```
old(john) :- true.
```

is the full version of the fact above. A fact is a rule whose body is the atom **true**. **true** is known by the interpreter, and when it is given as a goal it is immediately satisfied.

So facts and rules are structures of the same kind, in that both have the functor ':-'. The word *clause* is used to mean such a structure. So, for example, the database always contains a set of clauses.

Lists are also structures, although the notations given in Chapter 8 disguise this. Every non-empty list is a structure whose functor is '.'.

[H|T]	stands for	'.'(H,T)
[2]	stands for	'.'(2,[])
[3,4]	stands for	'.'(3,'.'(4,[]))

and so on. The empty list is denoted by []. [] is an atom, one of the special ones mentioned earlier.

This notation for lists emphasises that lists actually do fit into the scheme of Prolog terms, as structures. But in practice the notation which was introduced earlier, i.e. [H\|T], is rather more convenient, and you should continue to use it.

Quotation Marks

The use of *quotation marks* is a common source of confusion. As mentioned earlier, atoms may be bounded by single quotes. When it is required that an atom contain non-alphanumeric characters or start with an upper-case letter, the single quotes are essential. That is why in earlier chapters we used names beginning with lower-case letters, e.g **methuselah**, **john**, **jane**, **bill**. In some cases we used names starting with upper-case letters, e.g. in Chapter 7: **'Tanenbaum'**, **'March'**, but we had to accept the extra complication of the quotation marks. In Chapter 7 we also used non-alphanumeric characters in names, e.g. **'Prentice-Hall'**, **'Structured Computer Organization'**. Another situation where atoms occur as names is as names of files. When we gave the goal **?- [exam].** we relied on the name of the file being **exam**, a Prolog atom. But it is convenient for names of files to have suffixes, as in **marks.dat** or **exam.pro**. To load the contents of such a file, the name of the file must be made into an atom by enclosing in single quotes, e.g. **?- ['marks.dat'].**

One drawback to the use of atoms for names arises when reading and writing. Details are left to Chapter 14, but the problem is simply described. The goal

```
?- write('Hello user.').
```

will cause the message

```
Hello user.
```

to appear on the screen. However, it can also be used to write to a file, and when writing to a file, the quotation marks are not sent to the file. As a result, if subsequently an attempt is made to read at this point in the file, failure occurs, because `Hello user.` is not an atom (indeed it is not a Prolog structure at all). Some recent Prolog systems have surmounted this difficulty by including a special predicate **writeq** which writes the quotation marks in full.

Another awkwardness over quotation marks has perhaps been apparent in this text. One cannot use single quotes when referring to Prolog code, because they may affect the meaning. For example, the phrase

the variable `'X'`

does not make sense, because, although **X** is a variable, `'X'` is not a variable – it is an atom.

A standard alternative to single quotes is of course the use of double quotation marks. But Prolog has a special use for these also. Double quotes are used to represent *strings*. A string is in fact a list (as defined in Chapter 8) of ASCII codes for characters. The notation which uses double quotes is an alternative notation. A sequence of characters enclosed in double quotes is much easier to read than a Prolog list of character codes!

```
"hello"     stands for     [104,101,108,108,111].
```

Any characters are allowed in a string, but note that it is the ASCII codes which form the list. Try giving the goal

```
?- write("Hello user!").
```

to the interpreter. You will see one reason why strings do not provide an immediately convenient way to represent names.

Metalogical Predicates

Prolog variables may during a run be instantiated in various possible ways, and the programmer may require, at some point in the program, to check on the way that some variable has been instantiated. There are no types as such in Prolog, but here we are dealing with what in another language would be type information. The goal

```
?- atom(X).
```

succeeds if (the current value of) X is an atom. So

```
?- X = mary, atom(X).
```

will succeed. Of course the goal

```
?- atom(mary).
```

will also succeed, but in this explicit fashion, atom is unlikely to be very useful.

The goals

```
?- integer(X).
?- number(X).
```

can be used likewise to check on whether (the current value of) X is an integer or a number. A number in this context means any numerical value, including both integers and floating point numbers.

Lastly, the goals

```
?- var(X).
?- nonvar(X).
```

serve a similar purpose. The first of these checks on whether X is an uninstantiated variable (and succeeds if it is). The second will succeed if X is currently instantiated (to a value which is not itself an uninstantiated variable).

11 Matching, Equality

It is now time to give rather more detail about the process of matching which has been mentioned earlier, since it is an essential part of the way in which the Prolog interpreter works. The basic idea is that two terms can be matched if they can be made identical by giving values to variables occurring in them. This process of giving values to variables in order to match terms is called *instantiation*, and the process of matching always carries out the minimum amount of instantiation required. It is important to realise that this process is the *only* way in which variables take values.

Matching

There are three kinds of term: a constant, a variable and a structure, so when attempting to match two terms, one of the following six cases must apply.

1. Constant with constant. Here matching is impossible (and the process fails), unless the two constants are identical. Remember that the only constants are atoms and numbers.

2. Constant with variable. Here the variable becomes instantiated, i.e. it takes the constant as its value, and the matching process succeeds. Of course, this assumes that the variable is currently uninstantiated. If it has previously been given a value, then the matching process must use that value, not the variable itself.

3. Constant with structure. Such terms cannot be matched, so the matching process fails in this case.

4. Variable with variable. Here the two variables are made to 'share'. Out of sight of the user, the interpreter creates another variable and gives it as value to both of the original variables. The effect is that any subsequent instantiation of either of the two original variables will automatically be carried out on the other. Again, this assumes that neither variable has previously been instantiated.

63

5. Variable with structure. As in Case 2 above, the variable becomes instantiated, i.e. takes the structure as its value, and the match succeeds. Notice that the structure may itself contain further variables, which may subsequently become instantiated by the matching process.

6. Structure with structure. This is the most complex case. What happens may be described algorithmically as follows:

> IF the structures have the same functor and the same number of arguments
> THEN attempt to match all of the arguments separately in pairs
> ELSE the matching process fails

It may be helpful to illustrate Case 6 by means of examples. First, consider the two structures

```
child(X,Y)

child(mary,john)
```

These have the same functor and the same numbers of arguments, so the matching process will attempt to match separately

```
X with mary

Y with john.
```

Both of these will succeed (Case 2), causing X and Y to become instantiated, and the matching of the two given structures succeeds.

Second, consider the two structures

```
child(mary,Y)

child(jane,john)
```

These have the same functor and the same number of arguments, so the matching process will attempt to match separately

```
mary with jane

Y with john.
```

The first of these will fail (Case 1), so the matching of the two given structures fails.

The matching process is *recursive*. The arguments in a structure may themselves be terms of any kind, so when arguments are matched, any of the six cases could apply.

Exercise

Consider in detail the process of matching the following two structures.

```
event(date(Day,Month,Year),
      birth('John Smith',
            male,
            parents(Father,Mother)))

event(date(7,'March',1958),
      birth('John Smith',
            male,
            parents('James Smith','Mary Jones')))
```

The underscore has been mentioned earlier, and this is now perhaps the occasion to explain how the interpreter treats it (in particular, how the matching process treats it). The underscore is a special variable — when we met it before, we called it the anonymous variable. It never holds a value, but it can be matched with anything. So it has a special case all to itself:

7. Underscore with any term. Matching succeeds and no instantiation is made.

This is useful when we need to ensure that complex structures match without being concerned about some of the values held in them. For example, in the exercise above, replace the first structure by

```
event(date(_,_,_),
      birth('John Smith',
            male,
            parents(Father,Mother)))
```

Matching with the second structure given above will cause the variables **Father** and **Mother** to become instantiated, ignoring the date, but at the same time ensuring that the correct form of date structure is present.

Equality

Equality may be appropriately discussed at this point because, as we saw early on, goals which involve = call for terms to be *matched*. In this sense, = does not mean 'equals'. It means 'can be matched with'. Equality can be confusing in Prolog, because there are three different kinds:

65

=	'can be matched with'
==	'is identical to'
=:=	'evaluates to the same value as'

The third of these has been mentioned in Chapter 9. This is used only with arithmetic expressions, and does not involve the matching process.

The difference between = and == can be very significant. The == does not involve the matching process at all. It takes two terms and compares them as they are. So in this respect its meaning is closer to normal equality than is the meaning of =.

It should be remembered that when a sequence of subgoals is being satisfied, instantiations may take place which must be allowed for in subsequent matchings. Consider the following examples:

```
?- X = 5.
?- X == 5.
?- X is 3 + 2, X == 5.
?- X = john, X = 5.
```

The first is achieved (Case 2 of the matching process) and X is instantiated to 5. The second fails, because X (uninstantiated) is not identical with 5. The third succeeds — first of all X is given the value 5, and then the second part in effect becomes ?- 5 == 5. The fourth will fail, because X will be given the value john, and clearly john cannot be matched with 5 (Case 1). Try a few such goals for yourself and be sure that you understand what happens.

Most Prolog systems include the negations of the three kinds of equality:

\=	'cannot be matched with'
\==	'is not identical to'
=\=	'has value different from the value of'

These should be used with care, bearing in mind the meanings of the three different kinds of equality. And see the discussion of the built-in predicate **not** in Chapter 17.

12 Control Structures, Loops

The execution of a Prolog program is always under the control of the interpreter, with its standard mode of operation — matching, generating subgoals, backtracking. Prolog programs do not consist of sequences of instructions, so the kinds of control structure used in ordinary programming to carry out iterative or repetitive tasks (FOR loops, WHILE loops and REPEAT...UNTIL loops, for example) are not appropriate in Prolog. Nevertheless, the mechanisms of Prolog can be used to carry out repetitive operations, and this chapter shows how.

Failure-driven Loops

We have seen examples of Prolog's 'looping' facilities already in earlier chapters. Backtracking can cause looping in a fairly obvious way, according (for example) to the form

```
passed(Student) :-
        mark(Student,X),
        X > 49.
```

The body of this rule is in effect a rudimentary REPEAT...UNTIL loop, with X > 49 forming the terminating condition. To use backtracking in this way, the programmer must be able to see in advance:

1. where failure will occur (causing the backtracking) — failure at an unexpected place may destroy the proper functioning of the loop, and

2. which predicate(s) will be re-satisfied on backtracking, i.e. which point is in effect the beginning of the loop.

The other part of the same example from Chapter 5 provides simple illustration.

```
passlist :-
        passed(Student),
```

67

```
          write(Student), nl,
          fail.
    passlist.
```

The body of this rule is a loop. This time it is clear which subgoal will fail and cause the backtracking (the **fail**). But in order for the loop to work we have to know that the interpreter will not be able to re-satisfy the subgoal **nl** or the subgoal **write(Student)**, so that the loop takes control right back to **passed(Student)**, which is where we wish to proceed from. It is thus important to know, for any predicate, built-in or user-defined, whether it can be re-satisfied on backtracking. Appendix A contains a list of standard built-in predicates, and indicates which of them *can* be re-satisfied. In particular, **read** and **write** cannot be re-satisfied. We shall see in the next chapter one way to control this aspect of user-defined predicates.

The example of **passlist** above does not correspond with the RE-PEAT...UNTIL form, of course. The subgoal **fail** at the end of the loop body will cause looping *every time*. In this case the exit from the loop occurs when **passed(Student)** cannot be re-satisfied any further, and *it* fails. In this sense the structure here is more like that of a WHILE loop.

So far so good. But here is a difficulty. It is not uncommon to wish to carry out a looping algorithm whose body consists of (say)

```
    read(Data)
    process(Data,Output),
    write(Output)
```

Using a failure-driven loop we might write an example of a program with this structure like this:

```
    doubles :-
          read(X),
          Y is X * 2,
          write(Y), nl,
          fail.
    doubles.
```

Try this for yourself, and note that no looping takes place. The **fail** causes backtracking, but none of the other subgoals in the body of the rule can be re-satisfied. We would like **read(X)** to read in more data, but it cannot. Prolog allows us to cope with this problem by means of the built-in predicate **repeat**, whose sole function is to stand at the beginning of such loops. **repeat**, when given as a goal, always succeeds, and is re-satisfied whenever the backtracking process returns to it. It has no other effect. So try this now:

```
doubles :-
        repeat,
        read(X),
        Y is X * 2,
        write(Y), nl,
        fail.
doubles.
```

There is still something wrong with this, as you will discover if you try
it. It will loop for ever. There is no way out of the loop, either from the
beginning of the loop body or from the end. But this would be a problem
we would have to face whatever language we were using. There would have
to be some criterion specified for coming out of the loop. For example:

1. read and write 100 numbers,

2. read and write until the number read is 0,

3. build in to the loop a request to the user whether to continue or not.

The first of these is not easy to program in Prolog (it would be easily
implemented by means of an ordinary iterative loop in most languages).
The second and third are easier, but care is needed to make things tidy.
You should try the third as an exercise, but do not try the first yet. It
needs recursion rather than a failure-driven loop. Here is a solution for the
second.

```
doubles :-
        repeat,
        read(X),
        Y is X * 2,
        write(Y), nl,
        X = 0.
```

This is now even more like a REPEAT loop. But note that it still suffers
from the disadvantage that the terminating value (0) still gives rise to a
computation and an output. Can you rewrite the definition of doubles so
as to avoid this? You may need to make use of the semicolon.

Care is necessary when using repeat. It should not be used when the
start of the loop is a subgoal which *can* be re-satisfied on backtracking.
Think about what the effect of the following would be:

```
passed(Student) :-
        repeat,
        mark(Student,X),
        X > 49.
```

69

Convince yourself by trying it out.

Loops such as the ones which we are describing here can be nested. But of course it requires care over where failure occurs, and over where the interpreter will backtrack to. This aspect of program structure really requires the use of comments in the code to make clear to a reader what is intended.

Recursion

There is another way in Prolog of providing a looping mechanism, and that is using recursion. We saw a simple example when recursion was introduced in Chapter 4.

```
writenums(0) :- write(0).
writenums(N) :-
        write(N), nl,
        M is N - 1,
        writenums(M).
```

While this is definitely a recursive program, not an iterative looping program, it is formally similar to, and its effect is the same as, a program written in another language, involving a WHILE loop, e.g. (Pascal)

```
while n > 0 do
begin
    write(n);
    writeln;
    n := n - 1
end
```

Of course the same effect could be achieved in Pascal also by means of a program which is explicitly recursive. In Prolog, however, we do not have the same freedom. The recursive program is the only practical choice for this task.

We postponed consideration of the task of reading 100 numbers, doubling each and writing the results. Here now is a Prolog program to do this:

```
doubles(0).
doubles(N) :-
        read(X),
        Y is X * 2,
```

```
write(Y), nl,
M is N - 1,
doubles(M).
```

The variable **N** is a parameter which stands for the number of numbers whose doubles are still required. Try it!

Lists are very commonly used in Prolog for structured data items. Processing lists is therefore a common requirement in Prolog, and as we have observed before, recursion is the natural way to do this. Suppose that we wish to process each member of a given list, to obtain a new list. In Prolog we can do it thus:

```
convert([],[]).
convert([H|T],[H1|T1]) :-
        process(H,H1),
        convert(T,T1).
```

The predicate **process** may be anything, simple or complicated. For example, to double every number in the given list, use **convert** as above together with

```
process(X,Y) :- Y is X * 2.
```

13 Cut

Backtracking is an essential feature of Prolog. It is necessary for the programmer to understand it and to make use of it, and in earlier chapters we seen many examples of its beneficial use. But there are also drawbacks which must be recognised. First, it can lead to wrong answers, and second, it can lead to much wasted machine time. Before discussing the remedy, which is the subject of this chapter, let us try to pin down the problems.

The Problem of Wrong Answers

In Chapter 5 we saw the example:

```
/* To compute the larger of two numbers,
      here represented by X and Y */
max(X,Y,Y) :- X < Y.
max(X,Y,X) :- X >= Y.
```

We noted in Chapter 5 that the second rule contains a test which is strictly unnecessary. Let us consider now what would be the effect of simply removing that test, so that the definition becomes

```
max(X,Y,Y) :- X < Y.
max(X,Y,X).
```

This new version of **max** will behave correctly in some circumstances. If the rule fails, the fact will apply, and cause the third argument to be properly instantiated. So a goal `?- max(A,B,C).` where **A** and **B** are already instantiated to numerical values, will succeed, and the variable **C** will be given a value which is the larger of the values held by **A** and **B**.

This works fine in isolation. But when we need to use **max** within a larger program, things can go wrong. As a result of the workings of other goals, backtracking may take place, and such backtracking may encounter and attempt to resatisfy a subgoal involving **max**. There are two possible ways to achieve a **max** subgoal: using the rule and using the fact, and resatisfying can give wrong answers, as the following example shows.

```
/* Loop to read pairs of integers and
   display the larger of each pair    */
displaymax :-
        repeat,
        write('Enter X: '), nl, read(X),
        write('Enter Y: '), nl, read(Y),
        max(X,Y,Z),
        write('Larger is: '), write(Z), nl,
        X = 0.
```

The final subgoal (X = 0) is merely a simple-minded mechanism for leaving
the loop. It is very instructive actually to see how displaymax behaves, so
try it out for yourself. Try the values 5 for X and 3 for Y. It works fine.
Now try the values 3 for X and 5 for Y. Can you explain why both numbers
are written out? This will happen whenever the second number is larger
than the first. The problem is one which was alluded to in Chapter 12. In
a failure-driven loop we must be sure that backtracking will take us back
to the place which is intended to be the beginning of the loop. Here it does
not. When ?- X = 0. fails, backtracking occurs, but rather than return
to the repeat, the interpreter finds an intermediate subgoal which *can* be
re-satisfied, namely max(X,Y,Z). It can be re-satisfied by using the *fact* for
max (where the first time around it was the rule which was used). In cases
where the Y is not larger than the X, this difficulty will not arise because the
rule for max will fail the first time and the fact will be used instead (and so
on backtracking there will be no *further* way to achieve the max subgoal).

   Such difficulties may be obvious, as in the above case, or they may be
extremely subtle and hard to trace. In Chapter 8 a predicate member was
defined by

```
member(X,[X|_]).
member(X,[_|T]) :- member(X,T).
```

Now imagine a failure-driven loop, the body of which contains a subgoal of
the form ?- member(A,L). If the list L contains no repetitions then there
will be no difficulty, but if the value of A occurs in the list L more than once,
then the subgoal ?- member(A,L). can be re-satisfied on backtracking, thus
interfering with the functioning of the loop. To see this behaviour of member
explicitly, try (after loading the above definition of member) the goal

```
?- member(2,[3,2,1,2,4,2]),write('Found'),fail.
```

We shall see later in this chapter how we can adjust the definitions of
predicates such as max and member so as to avoid these difficulties.

The Problem of Wasted Effort

The other kind of difficulty mentioned above is the potentially wasteful 'blind search' nature of the backtracking process. The interpreter will try every avenue available in order to achieve a goal. It will certainly be advantageous to be able to restrict this search if we can, and there are two kinds of situation which might arise. One is: once a particular predicate has been satisfied, it may be appropriate to ensure that the interpreter never re-satisfies it. Another is: if the interpreter reaches a particular point in its efforts to achieve a goal and has not succeeded, it may be appropriate to enable it to give up without pursuing further fruitless search. The first of these is obviously related to the difficulties arising in the examples above. Let us consider the second kind of situation, therefore. The following example illustrates the point.

Suppose that the database contains a number of facts representing personal details of individual people: name, reference number, age, sex, marital status, say. One such fact might be

```
details(['Parry','George'],3471,57,male,married).
```

The task is to write a predicate which will find out whether a named individual has reached pensionable age, by reference to this database. Here is a suggestion:

```
pensionable(Person) :-
        details(Person,_,Age,Sex,_),
        old_enough(Age,Sex).

old_enough(A,male)   :- A > 64.
old_enough(A,female) :- A > 59.
```

Now consider what happens when the goal

```
?- pensionable(['Parry','George']).
```

is given to the interpreter. The first subgoal will be

```
?- details(['Parry','George'],_,Age,Sex,_).
```

The interpreter will scan the database, and will succeed in matching this goal with the details fact given above, causing Age to take the value 57 and Sex to take the value male. The second subgoal will now be

```
?- old_enough(57,male).
```

75

This will fail. Of course it is clear to *us* now that this person is not of pensionable age, and so the original goal should fail. But the interpreter does not know this yet. The backtracking process is initiated, and the interpreter returns to the goal

```
?- details(['Parry','George'],_,Age,Sex,_).
```

to try to re-satisfy it. This will involve comparing the goal with every fact for the predicate **details** which occurs in the database after the one which matched before. In a practical situation this might involve a large amount of checking, and all to no purpose, because we know that each individual has only one **details** fact. What we could use here is some way to tell the interpreter not to go looking for alternatives if the first one found is not suitable.

Of course the second sort of difficulty is not as serious as the first. It will not lead to wrong answers. And when learning to use Prolog it is not helpful to be too much distracted by consideration of efficiency. But it is something which a Prolog user needs to be aware of. In an application it could mean the difference between acceptable performance and unacceptable performance.

The Remedy

The *cut*, represented by the sign !, can occur as a subgoal at any point in the body of a rule. Formally, ! is one of the special atoms mentioned in Chapter 10. A ! subgoal is always immediately achieved (and cannot be re-satisfied on backtracking). At this level of the operation of the interpreter the cut has no effect at all. But the cut also affects the interpreter's subsequent behaviour in the ways which we now describe.

Consider again the **pensionable** example from above. Let us insert a cut as follows:

```
pensionable(Person) :-
        details(Person,_,Age,Sex,_), !,
        old_enough(Age,Sex).

old_enough(A,male)   :- A > 64.
old_enough(A,female) :- A > 59.
```

Now when the goal

```
?- pensionable(['Parry','George']).
```

is given, the sequence of events is:

76

1. `?- details(['Parry',George'],_,Age,Sex,_).` is achieved, giving
   `Age` the value 57 and `Sex` the value `male` (as before).

2. The `?- !.` subgoal is achieved.

3. The subgoal `?- old_enough(57,male).` fails, and the backtracking
   process is initiated.

4. The backtracking process encounters the !, and stops. No attempt is
   made to re-satisfy the subgoal

   `?- details(['Parry',George'],_,Age,Sex,_).`

   The original goal now fails without further ado.

This behaviour is, of course, exactly what we saw as desirable in the
earlier discussion. The cut acts rather like a turnstile, allowing passage
in only one direction. Once the interpreter has achieved the ! subgoal,
the backtracking process cannot go back through the cut, and unnecessary
checking does not take place. This is the primary function of the cut. It
limits backtracking by preventing any attempt to re-satisfy subgoals which
precede it in the body of the same rule.

But the cut does more than prevent backtracking among the subgoals
in a single rule. It also prevents the interpreter from seeking alternative
clauses. For example, if there had been other facts or rules for `pensionable`,
then the goal

   `?- pensionable(['Parry','George']).`

would have been treated exactly as described above. The cut would prevent
any attempt to achieve this goal in another way.

In attempting to satisfy complex goals, the interpreter may deal with
large numbers of subgoals, and may have to cope with failures occurring
often and at various depths in the nesting of the subgoals. It is important
to realise that the effects of the cut may not happen immediately — indeed they can come into play some considerable time after the cut itself
is achieved. The effect (preventing re-satisfaction of earlier subgoals or of
the parent goal) will occur when the backtracking process comes back to
the point of the cut, irrespective of how many other subgoals have been
achieved or how much backtracking has been carried out in the meantime.

Let us return now to our other example, `max`. Insert a cut in the abbreviated definition of `max` as follows.

```
max(X,Y,Y) :- X < Y, !.
max(X,Y,X).
```

The cut comes into play only in cases when a goal ?- `max(X,Y,Z)`. has been achieved through achieving the subgoal ?- `X < Y`. But then it will have an effect only if a subsequent failure (of some other subgoal) causes backtracking, and that backtracking returns to try to re-satisfy the ?- `max(X,Y,Z)`. goal. If the cut were absent, `max` could be re-satisfied by application of the second clause (the fact). The presence of the cut prevents this. With this cut in place, the predicate `displaymax` (see above) then works properly. The failure of ?- `X = 0`. causes backtracking as before, but this time the backtracking will take us straight back to the `repeat`, because the cut prevents `max` from being re-satisfied. Try it for yourself.

Of course, there is another way to fix `max`, namely to return to the original version, given in Chapter 5, in which both clauses are explicit:

```
max(X,Y,Y)  :- X < Y.
max(X,Y,X)  :- X >= Y.
```

But this contains the unnecessary test. Using the cut is rather more efficient, but makes for code which is harder to read.

Next, here is a 'fixed' version of `member`:

```
member(X,[X|_])  :- !.
member(X,[_|T])  :- member(X,T).
```

Note that the cut can stand on its own in the body of a rule. The effect of this is that, once a goal ?- `member(A,L)`. has been achieved, then backtracking caused by the subsequent failure of some other subgoal cannot cause the same ?- `member(A,L)`. to be achieved again, even if the value of A does occur more than once in the list L.

Uses of the cut can be extremely subtle, and, as with other features, it is only through experience that one learns to use it effectively. But here is another word of warning. Uses of the cut are a complication — they make programs harder to read. For this reason they should be thinly spread, and every occurrence of a ! should normally be explained by a comment.

Common Uses of the Cut

To end this chapter it will perhaps be useful to describe the effect of the cut in three specific kinds of situation.

- A cut at the end of the body of a rule. For example

```
pred :- a, b, c, d, !.
```

The effect of this is that after being achieved once by application of this rule, **pred** cannot be re-satisfied on backtracking. Our examples **max** and **member** are like this.

- A cut at the beginning of the body of a rule. For example

    ```
    pred :- !, a, b, c, d.
    ```

    The effect of this is that if the conjunction **a, b, c, d** fails, then **pred** fails, even if there are other clauses for **pred**.

- A cut in combination with **fail**. For example

    ```
    pred :- a, b, c, !, fail.
    ```

    The effect of this is (presuming that **a, b, c** are achieved) that ?- **pred.** fails, and no backtracking takes place at this level (i.e. in the attempt to achieve ?- **pred.**).

It is important to realise that the effects of a cut do not extend up to the next level of nesting of goals (if there is one). For example, suppose that **pred** is defined as in any of the above cases, and that we have another predicate whose definition includes a call to **pred**, e.g.

```
task :- g1, g2, pred.
task :- g3.
```

Then if, in an attempt to achieve the goal ?- **task.**, the subgoal ?- **pred.** eventually fails as a result of the cut mechanism, this will not prevent the interpreter from backtracking (at the level of **task**) to g2 and to g1, and even if necessary to g3.

14 Input/Output

From the beginning we have made use of **read** and **write**. These quite straightforwardly read and write Prolog terms of any kind from/to the terminal. The only points to bear in mind are:

1. An input term must be followed by a full stop and a carriage return.

2. When an atom enclosed in single quotes is written, the quotation marks do not appear.

3. When a string is written (consisting of characters enclosed in double quotes) it is the ASCII codes of the characters which appear.

4. Most systems have a limit on the number of characters allowed in an atom. The convenience of writing messages as atoms can be restricted by this.

5. **read** and **write** are not of much use for the input and output of *text*. This is because single characters are not legal Prolog terms. Dealing with text on a character-by-character basis therefore requires use of character codes and the predicates **get**, **get0** and **put**. These are dealt with below.

It is essential to realise that **read** and **write** will cope with an *entire* Prolog term in one operation. Achieving the goal **?- write(S).** will cause whatever term is the current value of the variable **S** to be written out in its entirety. Likewise, achieving the goal **?- read(S).** will cause whatever term is keyed in (provided that a syntactically correct term *is* keyed in) to be read and to be given as value to **S**. In particular, lists do not have to be read and written member-by-member.

In this Chapter we shall examine three aspects of input/output:

- file handling

- formatting

- reading and writing text

File Handling

Unless particular steps are taken (described below) the interpreter will always attempt to achieve **read** goals by reading from the terminal, and to achieve **write** goals by writing to the terminal screen. The 'normal' mode of operation is interactive with the user. The built-in predicates

```
see
seen
tell
told
```

provide the means to change this situation, so as to be able to read and write to or from files.

When we wish to read from a file called, say, **usefuldata**, we give the goal

```
?- see(usefuldata).
```

The name of the file must be an atom, so if the file's name is actually **usefuldata.dat**, then the argument which is given to **see** must be the atom **'usefuldata.dat'** (with quotation marks). Similarly if the name contains any non-alphanumeric characters. The effects of achieving such a goal are as follows:

1. The named file is opened (if it is not open already) for reading.

2. Subsequent **read** goals take data from this file.

If the named file does not exist then the **see** goal will fail. Otherwise it succeeds, and cannot be re-satisfied on backtracking.

When we are finished reading from the file, we give the goal

```
?- seen.
```

Note that this does not take the name of the file as an argument. The effect of achieving this goal is that the file which is currently being read from is *closed*, and the next input is taken from the terminal. It is perhaps useful to bear in mind the notion of 'the current input'. By default, the current input is the terminal. When required, the current input can be *switched* to (or between) files, by means of **see**, and can be returned to the terminal by means of **seen**. Here are some points to remember about **seen**:

1. After input has been completed, it is essential to revert to the terminal by means of **seen**.

82

2. If a file has been closed as a result of **seen**, then the next time the same file is opened for input it will be opened at the *beginning*.

3. The input can be switched to the terminal without closing the file currently being read from by giving the goal ?- **see(user)**. The name **user** denotes the terminal.

4. Several files can be open for reading at the same time, although only one can be associated with the current input. In such situations, the reading positions in the files are maintained and **see** goals can be used to switch the current input from one file to another. Only through the use of **seen** is the reading position lost, and then only in the file which is at that point the current input.

Examples

1.
```
ex1(A,B) :-
        see(file1),
        read(A),
        see(file2),
        read(B),
        seen.
```

The **seen** at the end is essential. After the goal ?- **ex1(A,B)**. has been achieved, the file **file1** remains open, but **file2** is closed.

2.
```
ex2(A,B) :-
        see(file1),
        read(A),
        seen,
        see(file1),
        read(B),
        seen.
```

As a consequence of achieving the goal ?- **ex2(A,B)**., the first item in the file **file1** will be read twice, and will be given as value to both **A** and **B**.

3.
```
ex3(A,B,C) :-
        see(file1),
        read(A),
        seen,
        read(B),
        see(file1),
        read(C),
```

```
                    seen.
```

Achieving the goal `?- ex3(A,B,C).` will cause `A` and `C` to take the same value (the first item in `file1`), and will cause `B` to be read from the terminal.

```
4.              ex4(A,B,C)  :-
                    see(file1),
                    read(A),
                    see(user),
                    read(B),
                    see(file1),
                    read(C),
                    seen.
```

This is different. The file `file1` will not be closed after the first `read`, so `C` will take the second item in the file as its value.

If you wish to experiment yourself with **see** and **seen**, you will need to construct some data files to be read from. Remember that **read** will read an entire Prolog term, provided that it is followed by a full stop and a non-printing character (normally a carriage return when reading from the terminal). The most convenient way to organise a data file, therefore, is to have a sequence of Prolog terms each followed by a full stop and a carriage return (i.e. each term on a separate line in the file). Here is a suggestion for two files to experiment with. Construct the files **odd** and **even** with the following contents:

```
odd:            1.
                3.
                5.
                7.
                9.

even:           2.
                4.
                6.
                8.
                10.
```

Incidentally, it is sensible to include a carriage return after the last full stop just to ensure that there is a non-printing character there.

The mechanism for directing output is based on the same principles as for input. Bear in mind the notion of 'the current output'. By default, the current output is the terminal and **write** goals will cause output to be sent to the screen. When required, the current output can be switched to (or between) files by using **tell**. For example we might give the goal

    ?- tell(fileforoutput).

where the argument for **tell** is the name of the appropriate file. This must be an atom, as with **see**. The effects of achieving a **tell** goal are:

1. The named file is opened for writing. If it does not already exist, it is created.

2. Subsequent **write** goals will send output to the named file.

3. If the named file exists and is not already open for writing, it is opened at the beginning.

4. If the named file is already open for writing (as a result of a previous **tell**), the current output is switched to this file and the next output will go to the current position in it.

As with **see**, a **tell** goal cannot be re-satisfied on backtracking.

Corresponding to **seen**, there is **told**. Achieving the goal

    ?- told.

will cause the file which is currently associated with the output to be closed, and the current output to be switched to the terminal. The four points made above about **seen** also apply (in the context of output rather than input, of course) to **told**. Note the availability of **?- tell(user)**. This allows switching of the output to the terminal screen without closing the file previously associated with the output, thus maintaining the position in that file.

Several files can be open for writing at the same time, although only one can be associated with the current output. This situation is exactly analogous to that for reading. In the middle of a large program which may involve reading or writing from or to several files, it can be convenient (even necessary) to find out at some particular stage, which file is currently associated with the input and/or the output. The built-in predicates

    seeing
    telling

allow us to do this. Achieving the goal

    ?- seeing(X).

will cause X to be instantiated to the name of the current input file. (This may of course be **user**.) Likewise, achieving the goal

```
?- telling(X).
```

will cause X to be instantiated to the name of the current output file. (Again, this may be **user**.)

Formatting

The facilities provided by Prolog are on most systems rudimentary only. The basic built-in predicates are

```
nl
tab
put
```

We have already seen **nl** in operation. We can now observe (trivially) that when writing to a file, **nl** will cause an end-of-line character to be written to the file.

Achieving the goal

```
?- tab(8).
```

causes eight spaces to be output. Any positive integer can be given as an argument to **tab**. Note that this provides *relative* tabulation only. There is no built-in facility for setting and using absolute tabulation points.

Lastly, **put**. Achieving the goal

```
?- put(N).
```

will cause the character whose ASCII code is N to be written to the current output. Obviously the argument to **put** must be an integer in the range 0...127 (or it may be a variable, provided that at the time the interpreter comes to the **put** goal, the variable has been given such an integer as its value).

As a simple (and necessary) exercise in formatting, let us consider the task of writing Prolog terms to a file in such a way that they can be read back again. Remember that **read** requires each term to be followed by a full stop followed by a non-printing character. Here is an example:

```
buildfile :-
        tell(even),
        write(2), put(46), nl,
```

```
        write(4), put(46), nl,
        write(6), put(46), nl,
        write(8), put(46), nl,
        write(10), put(46), nl,
        told.
```

Achieving the goal

```
    ?- buildfile.
```

will cause a file called **even** to be created, and the contents

```
    2.
    4.
    6.
    8.
    10.
```

to be inserted in it. Note that **46** is the ASCII code for a full stop. Both the **put(46)** and the **nl** are essential if this file is to be readable by means of the Prolog **read**.

A further complication arises when the Prolog terms being written are atoms enclosed in single quotes. As has been observed before, **write** will not reproduce the quotation marks. So for example, achieving the goal

```
    ?- write('First Record').
```

will cause **First Record** to be written. This cannot now be read, because it is not a Prolog term. Achieving the compound goal

```
    ?- put(39), write('First Record'), put(39).
```

will cause **'First Record'** to be written, and this is now in a form which can be read.

Combining both of the above ideas, consider

```
    buildatomfile :-
            tell(atomfile),
            put(39), write('First Record'), put(39),
            put(46), nl,
            put(39), write('Second Record'), put(39),
            put(46), nl,
            told.
```

Achieving the goal ?- **buildatomfile**. will cause two quoted atoms to be inserted into the file **atomfile**, so that the contents of the file will become

```
'First Record'.
'Second Record'.
```

This file has a format which is appropriate for reading.

Of course, if repeated use is to be made of such processes, new predicates should be defined for the task(s). For example

```
writequotedatom(A) :-
        put(39),
        write(A),
        put(39).

writeterm(T) :-
        write(T),
        put(46),
        nl.
```

On some Prolog systems there is already a built-in predicate called `writeq` which behaves just as `write` does, except that when writing an atom enclosed in single quotes, the quotation marks are reproduced. (`writeq` is rather more subtle than the above `writequotedatom`, therefore.)

Text

The problem with text is that the interpreter recognises only Prolog terms, and can store items of data only in the form of Prolog terms. And of course the built-in **read** and **write** take Prolog terms as their arguments. A piece of text, as such, is not a Prolog term, and cannot be fitted very easily into the form required.

We have seen one convenient way of *writing* text. A piece of text can be enclosed in single quotes (thus making it into an atom, which of course is a Prolog term) and then **write** will write it out so that it looks like text (i.e. without the single quotes). This way of working is appropriate for writing out messages such as prompts, error messages or menus. But it is limited to short pieces of text because most systems have a maximum length for an atom, for example 255 characters. Of course, longer sections of text can be broken up into several atoms which may be written separately, but this is not very handy.

The situation regarding input is rather different. We cannot expect input to be nicely represented as Prolog atoms for us. So we are thrown back to basics — dealing with text one character at a time. We have already seen the Prolog representation of characters by means of their ASCII codes.

Indeed we have already seen a way to output a single character, by means of **put**. For character-by-character input, Prolog provides three predicates:

```
get
get0
skip
```

Achieving the goal

```
?- get(X).
```

will cause X to be instantiated to the ASCII code of the next *printing* character on the current input. The variable X must be previously uninstantiated, i.e. it must currently hold no value. Achieving the goal

```
?- get0(X).
```

will cause X to be instantiated to the ASCII code of the next character of any kind on the current input. And last, achieving the goal

```
?- skip(X).
```

when X is already instantiated to a number (the ASCII code of a character), will cause the input to move on to the character following the next occurrence of the character whose code is the value of X.

Such goals can be achieved once, and cannot be re-satisfied on backtracking. And remember, of course, that they will cause the reading position on the current input to *move on*, and this effect is not undone on backtracking.

Note that **get** and **get0**, like **put**, deal with ASCII codes of characters, so their arguments will be given integers as values (in the range 0...127).

Example

Here is a definition of a predicate **show**, which will display the contents of any text file on the terminal screen.

```
show(F) :-
        see(F),      /* file to be displayed */
        tell(user),  /* write to the screen */
        repeat,
        get0(X),
        put(X),
        X = 26,      /* test for end-of-file */
        !,
        seen.
```

89

This example illustrates also, of course, the output of text, one character at a time, using **put**. Make sure that you understand how the loop works (see Chapter 12) and why the cut is there (Chapter 13).

Let us end this chapter with a reminder that the trouble with text is that Prolog cannot treat it as a Prolog term or even a combination of terms, so text cannot be stored by the interpreter as text. Conversion of text into a form suitable for the interpreter to store it and process it is quite a complicated task, which we shall not deal with. The interested reader may refer to the book 'Programming in Prolog', by Clocksin and Mellish, where a predicate **readin** is defined with just this purpose in mind.

15 Organising the Database

Consult and Reconsult

In earlier chapters we have seen how to load facts and rules into the database by means of the forms of goal

```
?- [user].
?- [anyfile].
```

These forms are in fact abbreviated forms of the following:

```
?- consult(user).
?- consult(anyfile).
```

The effect of a consult is to *add* facts and rules (clauses) to the database. We shall now concern ourselves more generally with ways of *changing* the database. First, there is a variation on consult which is very useful. Achieving the goal

```
?- reconsult(user).
```

has the effect of allowing the user to key in clauses, just as with consult, but with the following difference. The new clauses are stored in the database *in place of* any clauses which may already be there for the same predicates. Such clauses are lost. Existing clauses for other predicates are unaffected. So reconsult allows us to change what the database contains for any particular predicate. It is possible also to reconsult a file. Most systems have an abbreviated form for reconsult:

```
?- [-user].
?- [-anyfile].
```

or

```
?- [$user].
?- [$anyfile].
```

As a digression, let us mention here another useful feature of consult and reconsult. We are accustomed to dealing with facts and rules, either keyed in or taken from a file. But consult and reconsult can also deal with *goals*. If a consult comes across a goal, an attempt is made there and then to achieve that goal. To illustrate the usefulness of this, here is a situation which is not uncommon. Before running a particular Prolog program, it may be appropriate to consult a number of files containing program code, then to consult a number of files containing data (as Prolog facts, of course), and then to write out some prompt, menu or other message on the screen. All this can be done as follows. Construct a 'setup' file, containing (say)

```
?- consult(progfile1).
?- consult(progfile2).
?- consult(datafile1).
?- consult(datafile2).
?- consult(datafile3).
?- write('Key in ''go.'' to start.').
```

Then to initialise the run, only the goal

```
?- [setup].
```

need be given.

Adding and Deleting

Prolog has facilities which allow the addition and deletion of individual clauses (facts or rules) to or from the database. This can be a useful, sometimes essential, operation. The built-in predicates for this are:

```
assert
asserta
assertz
retract
```

Achieving the goal

```
?- assert(child(mary,john)).
```

will cause the fact

```
child(mary,john).
```

to be added to the database. Subsequently it will have exactly the same status as all of the other clauses in the database.

A new rule can also be asserted. Achieving the goal

```
?- assert((parent(X,Y) :- child(Y,X))).
```

will cause the rule

```
parent(X,Y) :- child(Y,X).
```

to be added to the database. Note the extra parentheses around the new rule in the **assert** goal. These are necessary on some systems for the interpreter to recognise the argument of **assert** as a single structure (the structure `':-'(parent(X,Y),child(Y,X))` in this case).

The argument to **assert** may (in the text of a program) be a variable. When the interpreter deals with it, however, the argument must have a value which has the correct form, namely either a rule or a term which can stand as a fact. Provided that its argument has the correct form, an **assert** goal will succeed immediately, and cannot be re-satisfied on backtracking.

Because of the way that the interpreter works (it always matches a goal with the *first* appropriate fact or rule it can find in the database), the order in which clauses are held in the database can be significant. Prolog does provide a certain amount of control over this, through the built-in predicates

```
asserta
assertz
```

Achieving the goal

```
?- asserta(X).
```

causes the clause X to be inserted at the beginning of the database. Achieving the goal

```
?- assertz(X).
```

causes the clause X to be added at the end of the database.

The **assert** facility (in conjunction with **retract**, described below) allow the database to be treated as *dynamic* entity, i.e. one which can be changed at will. As such, it is in principle no different from a machine memory. Indeed it could be used to simulate a machine memory, say by having atoms as identifiers and a predicate **val** (say) which associates identifiers with values. Changing the value of an identifier would be achieved by removing a fact from the database and inserting a new one, for example by removing

```
val(price,15).
```

and inserting

```
val(price,16).
```

This kind of use of the database should be avoided, however, for two reasons. First, Prolog works in a way very different from normal imperative languages. Importing into it some unsympathetic features of imperative languages goes against both its rationale and its design. And second, such use of the database is *very inefficient*. For this reason alone, changing the database in the ways described in this chapter should be done as infrequently as possible.

To remove a clause from the database, we may use **retract**. Achieving the goal

```
?- retract(child(mary,john)).
```

will simply remove the fact `child(mary,john).` from the database. So **retract** undoes **assert**. But **retract** behaves also in rather different ways which it is essential to understand. It can work even if its argument is not fully instantiated. The argument requires only to be sufficiently instantiated so that the predicate in the head of the clause is recognisable. The **retract** will then cause removal of the first clause which matches the given argument. For example, achieving the goal

```
?- retract(child(X,john)).
```

will have the effect of removing from the database the first fact which matches with `child(X,john)`. If there are none, then this goal will fail. If there is (at least) one, then X will become instantiated. For example, the fact which is removed might be

```
child(mary,john).
```

in which case X will take the value **mary**.

One consequence of the behaviour of **retract** is that it is reasonable for **retract** to have another particular property, namely that it *can* be re-satisfied on backtracking. For example, suppose that we have

```
removechildren(P) :-
        retract(child(X,P)),
        fail.
removechildren(P).
```

Then achieving the goal

```
?- removechildren(john).
```

will cause all of the facts which record children of john to be deleted. Of course the facility to re-satisfy **retract** may be used more subtly than this. There may well be circumstances in which we wish to remove some but not all clauses of a certain form.

Besides the basic **retract**, there will customarily be a built-in facility for removing all clauses either for a given predicate or which match a given structure. The precise forms vary from one system to another, but here are two which may be found.

```
?- retractall(X).
```

Achieving this will remove from the database all clauses which match with (the value of) **X**.

```
?- abolish(X,N).
```

Achieving this will remove from the database all clauses for the predicate with name **X** (**X** must be an atom), and number of arguments **N** (**N** must be a non-negative integer).

In normal operation, the database is hidden from the user, and (as has been stressed before) temporary. The built-in predicate **listing** can be used both to reveal and to save the database if required. Achieving the goal

```
?- listing(child).
```

will cause all clauses held in the database for the predicate **child** to be displayed. The format may not be quite the same as it was in the version which was originally inserted (via a **consult** or by **assert**), and the names used for variables will be names invented by the interpreter, but the clauses should be recognisable, and they are given in the order in which they are held. The clauses for any specified predicate may be inspected, using **listing**.

Next, it is not difficult to see now how to save the contents of the database in a file. In Chapter 14 we saw how to send output to a file using **tell**. This can be used just as well in conjunction with **listing**. Achieving the goal

```
?- tell(childfile), listing(child), told.
```

will cause all of the clauses for the predicate **child** to be written to the file **childfile**, in a form which allows this file to be subsequently consulted. Normally there is no way to save (all at once) the entire contents of the database. It has to be done one predicate at a time.

Example

```
reversefacts :-
        retract(child(X,john)),
        asserta(child(X,john)),
        fail.
reversefacts.
```

Achieving the goal ?- **reversefacts**. will cause the order of the facts held for children of **john** in the database to be reversed. You should make sure that you understand how this works, if necessary by following through by hand the sequence of steps taken if the database initially contains the facts

```
child(mary,john).
child(jane,john).
child(bill,john).
```

We used **asserta** in the definition of **reversefacts**. What would have happened if we had had **assertz** instead?

Example

```
assemblechildren(P,L)  :- makelist(P,[],L).

makelist(P,S,L) :-
        retract(child(X,P)), !,
        makelist(P,[X|S],L),
        asserta(child(X,P)).
makelist(P,L,L).
```

This is quite tricky. Achieving the goal

```
?- assemblechildren(john,Clist).
```

will cause the variable **Clist** to be given as value a list containing all of the (known) children of **john** (in our example, **Clist** will take the value [bill,jane,mary]). In **makelist** the argument S stands for the list of children found so far, which is passed in to the recursive call along with the next child found (the current X). When all of the **child** facts have been retracted, the **retract** goal fails, causing the **makelist** fact to be used to give the original variable **Clist** (which has been carried in to all of the recursive calls of **makelist** without being instantiated at all) the value required. The **asserta** goals then re-insert the original facts as the recursion unwinds. The cut prevents re-satisfaction. One thing to note is that the list of children generated is in reverse order to the order of the facts originally in the database.

One might wonder, with regard to this example, whether all of the retracting and asserting are really necessary. If all we need is to get the next child (the next value of X) each time round in `makelist`, would not

```
assemblechildren(P,L) :- makelist(P,[],L).

makelist(P,S,L) :-
        child(X,P), !,
        makelist(P,[X|S],L).
makelist(P,L,L).
```

have done just as well? Answer: no, this does not work. See if you can work out why. The reason is quite an important aspect of recursion. Try it out on the machine and see what happens.

Both of the examples above can be parameterised so that they may be applied to facts for some predicate to be supplied as an argument. But in order to do this we shall need the ideas of the next chapter, in particular on constructing goals.

Tailpiece

Let us conclude this chapter with mention of another built-in predicate which has to do not so much with organising the database as with making use of it. Normally, we would rely on the interpreter to find its own way around the database, by means of its standard procedure for trying to achieve goals. Sometimes it can be useful to take some of the control of this process away from the interpreter, by using the predicate `clause`. And `clause` has the additional feature that it enables us to break a clause down into its head and its body. We give `clause` two arguments, and these will be matched with the head and body of a rule. For example, suppose that the database contains

```
member(X,[X|_]).
member(X,[_|Y]) :- member(X,Y).
```

Then achieving the goal

```
?- clause(member(A,B),Z).
```

will cause `member(A,B)` to be matched with `member(X,[X|_])` and Z to be matched with `true` (so that A will share with X, B will take value `[X|_]`, and Z will take the value `true`). Remember that a fact is just a special kind of rule — one whose body is **true**. On backtracking, **clause** *can* be re-satisfied. In this example, re-satisfying the goal

```
?- clause(member(A,B),Z).
```

will cause **A** to share with **X**, **B** to be instantiated to **[_|Y]**, and **Z** to take the value **member(X,Y)**. The first time round, **clause** finds a match with the fact for **member**, and the second time round it finds a match with the rule. One thing to remember is that the first argument to **clause** must be sufficiently instantiated for the predicate in the head of the rule sought to be recognisable.

16 Building and Dismantling Structures

Consider the task: to remove from the database all facts for a given functor and with a given number of arguments. (This is a restricted version of 'abolish', described in Chapter 15.) For this we need to define a predicate, remove, say, with two arguments: the name of the predicate (an atom) and the number of arguments. We shall have to use retract in our definition, so somehow we shall have to construct the appropriate argument for retract. This must be such that it matches with the facts which we wish to remove. In the rule for remove, the name of the predicate in question will be represented by a variable (which is in effect a parameter), *but* we cannot write a structure with a variable as its head. That would be syntactically incorrect, irrespective of the actual value which the variable may have at runtime. See the rules given in Chapter 10 and the description of the matching process in Chapter 11. Precisely what we need is a way of referring to 'a structure whose functor is (the current value of) F, with N arguments, all of which are variables'. The built-in predicate functor does just this for us. Achieving the goal

```
?- functor(S,F,N).
```

where S is uninstantiated, will cause S to become instantiated to a structure whose functor is (the value of) F and which has N arguments, all of them variables. So

```
remove(F,N) :-
        functor(S,F,N),
        retract(S),
        fail.
remove(F,N).
```

will serve our purpose.

The problem mentioned in the Chapter 15, to reverse the order of the facts held for a given predicate (with given number of arguments) can now be solved also.

```
reversefacts(F,N) :-
        functor(S,F,N),
        retract(S),
        asserta(S),
        fail.
reversefacts(F,N).
```

Another use for **functor** is 'in reverse'. If S is already instantiated to a structure, and F and N are uninstantiated, then achieving the goal

```
?- functor(S,F,N).
```

will cause F and N to be instantiated (respectively) to the functor of S (an atom) and the number of arguments in S. In summary,

```
functor(S,F,N)
```

means 'S is a structure whose functor is F with number of arguments N'.

A similar facility is provided by the built-in predicate **arg**. Achieving the goal

```
?- arg(N,S,A).
```

where N and S must be instantiated to a number and a structure respectively, will cause A to become instantiated to the Nth argument in S. For example, achieving the goal

```
?- arg(2,child(mary,john),X).
```

will yield X = john. In summary,

```
arg(N,S,A)
```

means 'the Nth argument in the structure S is A'.

There is a third predicate available which performs a function similar to that of **functor** and **arg**. This is =.. (sometimes referred to as 'univ'). This is defined as an infix operator, so its mode of use is as follows. Achieving the goal

```
?- child(mary,john) =.. L.
```

will cause L to be instantiated to the list [child,mary,john]. Thus =.. can be used to take apart a structure, yielding a list. When it is used in this way, the structure on the left-hand side need not be fully instantiated, but its functor must be known. So achieving

```
?- child(X,Y) =.. L.
```

100

will yield L = [child,X,Y]. We can also use =.. in the other direction, to create a structure from a given list of components. Achieving

```
?- S =.. [child,mary,john].
```

will yield S = child(mary,john). The list on the right-hand side of the =.. must have an atom as its first member, but otherwise can contain any Prolog terms.

The three predicates **functor**, **arg** and =.. can be used to construct or destruct structures. One of our examples above has shown how a structure, once built, can be supplied to **retract** as an argument. But there is no limitation on what can be done with such 'built-up' structures. They can even be given as goals to the interpreter. We illustrate this by an example.

Example

There are nine students in a class, and they are separated out into three groups of three. This grouping information is held in the form of Prolog facts:

```
group1(brown).
group1(page).
group1(webster).
group2(frame).
group2(lucas).
group2(white).
group3(cook).
group3(nelson).
group3(stewart).
```

The predicate **grouplist** (defined below) is to be used to display a list of the names of the members of a given group.

```
grouplist(G) :-
        S =.. [G,Student],
        call(S),
        write(Student), nl,
        fail.
grouplist(G).
```

The variable G is to be a group name (e.g. **group2**). When the goal

```
?- grouplist(group2).
```

101

is given, first of all S takes as its value the structure group2(Student).
Then the subgoal ?-call(S) has the effect of giving this structure to
the interpreter as a subgoal. It is achieved by matching with the fact
group2(frame)., and then the name frame is written. The fail causes
backtracking to the call(S) subgoal, and so on in familiar fashion.

Prolog can construct and dismantle on a different level as well. It can
split atoms! The built-in predicate name relates atoms with corresponding
strings (i.e. lists of character codes). For example, achieving

```
?- name(john,L).
```

will cause L to take the value [106,111,104,110] (which can also be written as "john"). And in reverse, achieving

```
?- name(A,[109,97,114,121]).
```

or

```
?- name(A,"mary").
```

will cause A to take the value mary. This is a facility which is not often
used, but can be invaluable in certain contexts. One might be to build
predicate names from specified components. For example, take two given
atoms and concatenate them to form a new atom.

```
atomconcat(A1,A2,A)  :-
        name(A1,L1),
        name(A2,L2),
        append(L1,L2,L),
        name(A,L).
```

Here append is as we have defined it before. See for example Chapter 8.

17 Fail, True, Not

We have already come across **fail** and its principal use, in the construction of loops. It is a very simple predicate. A goal

```
?- fail.
```

is not achieved. That is all there is to it. Here are some examples.

1.   `pred(X) :- process(X), fail.`
                `pred(X).`

2.   `pred(X) :- process(X), !, fail.`

3.   `pred(X) :- process(X); fail.`

The first is a standard looping structure, with an additional fact causing eventual success. The second is not a loop — here the **!**, **fail** combination stops the backtracking (so `?- pred(X).` fails). The third is rather silly — the inclusion of the **;** **fail** has no effect whatever. Make sure that you understand why this is so.

Remember that while **fail** as a goal is simple, the consequences of failure are not always simple, because failure always causes backtracking.

The predicate **true** is even simpler, because there is no connection with the backtracking process. A goal

```
?- true.
```

is achieved immediately (and is not re-satisfied on backtracking). It figures implicitly in all facts, because a fact is just a rule whose body consists of **true**. It can also be of use in programs. For example

```
pred(X) :- process(X); true.
```

This form of body for the rule will ensure that a goal `?- pred(X).` will always succeed, whether by the success of **process(X)** or after the failure of **process(X)**. The same effect can of course be obtained by:

```
pred(X) :- process(X).
pred(X).
```

Now for **not**. In Chapter 1 we noted a significant practical limitation about the way that Prolog works. In Prolog there is no such thing as 'don't know'. If Prolog doesn't know then it responds with **no**. The only possible responses to a goal are 'yes, I can achieve this' and 'no, I cannot achieve this'. We must bear this in mind in the way that we use **not**. If the interpreter is given the goal

```
?- not(child(mary,john)).
```

what happens is that the interpreter will try to achieve the goal

```
?- child(mary,john).
```

If this succeeds, then the original (negated) goal fails. Otherwise the original goal succeeds. So the **not** is not a *logical* 'not' — it is an operational (success/failure) version. In some cases, of course, these are the same notion. The goal

```
?- not(3 < 2).
```

will succeed, because **?- 3 < 2.** fails, because **3 < 2** is actually false. On the other hand, the goal

```
?- not(child(alex,john)).
```

will succeed in a situation where **child(alex,john)** is not known, i.e. cannot be deduced from facts and rules in the database (irrespective of whether it is true or false).

We have seen an implicit use of **not** already, in Chapter 11. There the built-in predicates \=, \== and =\= were described. Any use of these is equivalent to an alternative formulation, using **not**.

```
?- X \= Y.    is equivalent to   ?- not(X = Y).
?- X \== Y.   is equivalent to   ?- not(X == Y).
?- X =\= Y.   is equivalent to   ?- not(X =:= Y).
```

It may be of interest to note that the behaviour of **not** is exactly as though it were defined as follows:

```
not(X) :- call(X), !, fail.
not(X).
```

You should try to understand this, as it is a useful illustration of **call** and of the **!**, **fail** combination.

Finally, here is a word of warning about **not** (and about failure in general). Failure causes backtracking. While constructive use can be made of backtracking, it is certainly desirable to avoid it where we do not want it. Controlling unwanted backtracking should not be a predominant aspect of programming in Prolog. So avoid unnecessary failures. They make programs harder to write, harder to maintain and harder to understand.

18 Debugging

The normal mode of working in Prolog is (in outline) as follows.

1. Build a file (or files) containing a program (using an editor).

2. Enter the Prolog system.

3. Consult the file(s) containing the program.

4. Have the Prolog interpreter attempt to achieve the top-level goal of the program.

Both the third and fourth stages of this process are stages at which errors may become apparent. Let us deal with the third stage first.

The `consult` will check the syntax of the program, i.e. that it consists of well-formed clauses which can be asserted into the database. Such syntax checking is similar in nature to the checking carried out by compilers for languages of other kinds. Below is a list of points to note about this checking process and its results.

- For each error found, a message is displayed showing the nature of the error and the position where it was detected.

- The point where an error is recognised may be after (perhaps substantially after) the point where the error actually occurred. The message given by the interpreter therefore may not be very helpful, and some detective work may be required.

- One syntax error can disturb the syntax of the whole of the rest of the program. The number of errors found and reported by the interpreter may therefore be very much larger than the actual number of errors. So correct the first error before expending effort on pinning down subsequent errors. They may just disappear.

- Goals involving `consult` and `reconsult` will always succeed (provided that the file in question exists), whether or not syntax errors are found. Bear in mind that any clauses found before a syntax error is detected *will* be properly added to the database.

- Be careful to terminate comments correctly. If this is not done, some of the code may be taken as part of a comment without any indication that this has happened.

- Typographical errors may not be recognised as syntax errors. For example, if the full stop at the end of a rule is typed as a comma, and there is a fact following the rule, then the fact will be regarded by the interpreter not as a fact but as part of the body of the rule. This kind of error can be hard to detect.

- If there is a syntax error in the very last clause in the file, that error may not be reported, and the `consult` may apparently be entirely successful, except that, of course, the incorrect last clause will not have been transferred into the database. For obvious reasons, this kind of error can be hard to detect also.

- If you use a built-in predicate but give it the wrong number of arguments, this will be picked up as a syntax error. On the other hand, if you use any other predicate with the wrong number of arguments, this will pass the syntax check.

- If you misspell a predicate name or use a predicate which has not been defined, this will not be detected by the syntax check.

- For the names of user-defined predicates, any atoms may be used, except those which are already used by the Prolog system for some particular purpose. It may not always be clear which atoms are disallowed by this, and you may have to change some names occasionally when the interpreter objects.

But all this is not really what this chapter is about. In many ways the points made above apply to the detection of errors in any computer language. The unusual feature of Prolog is the way in which it is executed, and this is the chief source of difficulty for programmers who are new to the language. It is very easy in Prolog to write a program which looks correct, and *is* syntactically correct, but which fails either to run in the manner intended or to produce the results expected. Prolog therefore provides some facilities for runtime debugging, to enable the user to see all or some of the sequence of steps which the interpreter takes in attempting to achieve given goals.

The basic feature of the debugging facilities on all systems is the *trace*. A trace is a representation in sequence of all of the subgoals which the interpreter attempts to achieve, with indication of which ones succeed, and (implicitly or explicitly) information about instantiations which are made.

The actual information provided, the format of the information, and the form of control which the user can exercise over the production of the trace, all vary from system to system. Here, therefore, we shall deal only with the simplest basic facilities. You should read your system manual or just experiment with your system in some of the ways described below, in order to find out more details.

First, at any time during execution we can *interrupt* the interpreter, by means of the standard system interrupt (which may be CTRL-C). This will cause execution to stop, and a prompt to be displayed. A single character response is expected to this, and keying **h** (followed by RETURN) will cause a list of the options to be displayed. These may include:

a	abort execution
b	break (see below)
c	creep (single-step)
e	exit from Prolog
h	help
l	leap to next spy point (see below)
n	notrace (switch off tracing)
s	skip to end of current subgoal
t	trace (switch on tracing)

In addition just keying RETURN in response to the prompt may cause the interpreter to resume as though there had been no interruption.

Second, we can switch tracing on and off when at the level of the ?-prompt. On some systems the goals

```
?- trace.
```

```
?- notrace.
```

have this effect. On other systems more subtle features are provided. But in any event a full trace is unlikely to be useful. It will be very long, and examining the whole of it will be extremely time-consuming. Sometimes we may have to view the whole trace to track down an error, but frequently we may have some idea of which predicates are the most suspect, and there is a standard facility which allows us to restrict the trace accordingly. This is the built-in predicate **spy**, which we now describe.

Achieving the goal

```
?- spy(pred).
```

109

will cause a *spy point* to be set on each clause held in the database for the predicate **pred**. The argument to **spy** must be the name of a predicate, and so must be an atom. The effect of a spy point is that during execution of a subsequent goal, whenever a clause is invoked which has a spy point attached to it, the interpreter will stop, just as though it had been interrupted. This gives the user an opportunity, as described above, to choose how to proceed. For example, we may wish to see the entire trace from that point on, or we may wish to see only the trace of the operation of that particular predicate, or we may decide that we do not wish to see the trace at that point, and so choose to *leap* to the next spy point. Spy points can be placed on as many predicates as we wish.

Of course, spy points are merely a debugging aid. They do not affect the result of running a program. But they should be removed once the program is performing satisfactorily, and before it is actually used. To remove spy points we use **nospy**. Achieving the goal

```
?- nospy(pred).
```

will remove spy points from all clauses for **pred**. To remove all spy points from the whole program, give the goal

```
?- nodebug.
```

As a further aid, there is **debugging**. Giving the goal

```
?- debugging.
```

causes a list of the current spy points to be displayed.

Customarily, the predicates **spy** and **nospy** are known to the interpreter as operators. The effect of this (see Chapter 19) is to allow an alternative syntax, without parentheses around the arguments. For example

```
?- spy pred.
```
```
?- nospy pred.
```

A program can fail to perform properly at runtime in three different ways. It can crash, or it can run indefinitely without apparently doing anything, or it can give wrong or unexpected results. The most frequent causes of a crash are:

- Attempting to read beyond the end of a file.

- A recursion which does not terminate properly, so that the burden of many recursive calls causes the interpreter to run out of space.

110

- A system-imposed time limit on attempts to prove goals. Generally, if there is such a limit, it is unlikely to be low enough to affect the running of a correct program.

The most frequent cause of failure to terminate is:

- An infinite loop, caused either by backtracking or by recursion. The latter may or may not cause space problems resulting in a crash, depending on the nature of the recursive predicate.

Of course, wrong or unexpected results can be produced in any number of ways, and it is impossible to make any general comments about this situation.

When a program crashes, a message is displayed, which may be followed by [break], and then followed by the ?- prompt. The *break* is a feature of Prolog which has not yet been discussed, and is applicable generally, not just in this context. A break causes execution to be suspended and a completely new Prolog interpreter to be started. This allows the user to modify the database, set or remove spy points, check the contents of the database, or indeed anything else that a Prolog interpreter can do. After a break, to return to the interpreter whose operation was suspended, just key in an end-of-file character (CTRL-Z). This will kill off the second interpreter completely, and the original interpreter will resume from the state it had been in when it was suspended. Recall from above that the break was one of the options usually allowed when execution is interrupted by a spy point or a system interrupt. It is possible to break within a break, and some systems will show always the current level of nesting of breaks. If you wish to induce a break deliberately, giving the goal

```
?- break.
```

will achieve this.

It may happen that a break occurs without your being aware of it. Indeed this may not have any noticeable effect on anything you do subsequently, except the following. When you wish to exit from Prolog, you may find that the normal operation (e.g. by CTRL-Z) does not work. This may be because you had been inside a break, and you have merely come out of it. So repeating the normal exit operation (perhaps more than once) may take you out of Prolog. Alternatively, giving the goal

```
?- abort.
```

will cause termination of all current executions, and a return to the top-level (original) interpreter, irrespective of how deeply into nested breaks you might have been.

19 Operators

As we saw in Chapter 9, every legal expression in Prolog which is not a constant or a variable is a structure. A structure has a functor and arguments, and the standard format for this is the *prefix* format, with the functor placed first, followed by the arguments, enclosed in parentheses, separated by commas. We have also seen that for certain built-in predicates there is an alternative allowable representation, namely *infix* format, without any parentheses. Examples are the arithmetic operations and the clause former ':-'.

    2 + 3   means   +(2,3).

    head :- body   means   ':-'(head,body)

Such alternative notations are allowed (and recognised) because these predicates are known to the interpreter as *operators*. The interpreter has built-in knowledge of the forms of these notations. Just what sort of knowledge this is we shall see shortly.

Besides having such built-in operators, Prolog allows the user to instruct the interpreter to regard particular user-defined predicates as operators in a similar fashion. The built-in predicate **op** serves this purpose. We illustrate it first by looking at some of the built-in predicates. The information known to the interpreter about the operators + and > can be represented as follows:

    op(500,yfx,+)

    op(700,xfx,>)

The first argument to **op** gives the *precedence level* of the operator, the second gives the *type* of the operator, and the third is the operator itself (an atom). Let us consider the first two in turn.

Precedence levels determine how the interpreter is to make sense of expressions which are not made explicit by the use of parentheses. For example

    3 + 4 > 0

means

$$(3 + 4) > 0, \quad \text{i.e. } >(+(3,4),0)),$$

and not

$$3 + (4 > 0), \quad \text{i.e. } +(3,>(4,0))),$$

because > has higher precedence than +. Likewise

    p :- g1, g2

means

    ':-'(p, ',',(g1, g2)),

and not

    ',','(':-'(p, g1), g2),

because ':-' has higher precedence than ','.

It is because operators may be used without parentheses around their arguments that each operator must be given a precedence level. In any expression not containing parentheses, the operator with the highest precedence is the principal one (and so will be the functor), and the sub-expressions so determined will be its arguments.

Now we turn to the type of an operator. First of all we must observe that Prolog allows only operators which are either *unary* (one argument) or *binary* (two arguments). The type of an operator is a code which carries information of three kinds.

1. Whether the operator is unary or binary.

2. Whether the operator is to be written in prefix, infix or postfix form.

3. The associativity of the operator.

The code itself is a schematic representation of an expression in which f stands for the operator and x and y stand for arguments. Thus the codes fx and xf indicate unary operators, and the codes xfy, yfx and xfx indicate binary operators.

It is also clear from such codes what format is intended. For unary operators, fx indicates prefix form, and xf indicates postfix form. For binary operators, only infix form is allowed, and this is consistently indicated by the codes xfy, yfx and xfx. Here are some examples.

1. The goal former ?- is a prefix operator. Its code is fx.

2. not is a prefix operator. Its code is fx. Instead of

```
not(child(mary,john))
```

we may write

```
not child(mary,john)
```

3. + and > (whose codes are **yfx** and **xfx**, given above) are binary operators, and they may be used in infix format, without parentheses.

Now let us consider how the codes carry information about the associativity of operators. Such information is needed only for binary operators, and is represented by the use of the different letters **x** and **y** in the codes. Before seeing what the codes mean, first we should be clear what this information is and why it is required. Take the subtraction operator as an example. The expression

```
3 - 2 - 1
```

would normally be taken to have value 0. But subtraction is a binary operation, and there are two stages to this evaluation. First subtract 2 from 3, and then subtract 1 from the result. Or, we may think of the sense of this expression more clearly by writing it as

```
(3 - 2) - 1
```

It would not be entirely unreasonable to imagine a different process of evaluation for the expression 3 - 2 - 1. We might first subtract 1 from 2, and then subtract the result from 3, giving the result 2. This may be represented by

```
3 - (2 - 1)
```

By convention, a human computer would normally choose the first evaluation procedure, so the 'correct' result is 0. But before mechanical evaluation can be carried out, the system has to know which way to go about it, in the absence of parentheses.

The code for -, which is **yfx**, contains this information. In an expression without parentheses, the principal operator is the one with highest precedence. But there may not be such a one, uniquely. As in the example above, there may be more than one operator with the same (highest) precedence. We must be able to choose one of them as the principal operator. In the case of 3 - 2 - 1, the principal operator is the *second* occurrence of -, and consequently we may write this expression as (3 - 2) - 1. In general, wherever a - occurs, its right-hand argument is not allowed to have a minus sign in it (nor any other operator with the same precedence).

But its *left-hand* argument may have occurrences of such operators. This requirement is indicated by the letters **x** and **y** respectively in the code for an operator. To sum up, let us consider the three possible codes in turn.

The code **yfx** means that the operator is *left-associative*. An example shows the sense of this:

     7 - 3 - 2 - 1   means   ((7 - 3) - 2) - 1.

The code **xfy** means that the operator is *right-associative*. The semicolon (standing for 'or') is an example of this:

     g1; g2; g3; g4   means   g1; (g2; (g3; g4)).

The code **xfx** is rather different. Use of an operator with this code requires that there always is a unique operator of highest precedence. More particularly, an operator with this code can occur only once in an expression without parentheses. Examples of such operators are = and **is**.

The examples given above of built-in operators are standard ones. Unfortunately, however, the precedences and associativities of built-in operators may vary from one implementation of Prolog to the next. It is dangerous, therefore, to make assumptions about this. One case to note particularly is that of the comma and the semicolon. What does

     g1; g2, g3

mean? It could be

     (g1; g2), g3,

or it could be

     g1; (g2, g3),

depending on the relative precedence levels of the two operators. It is clearly crucial for a programmer to know which it is.

If your system does not have a manual with this information clearly given for the built-in operators, then you can (laboriously) find it out, using **display**. This is a built-in predicate which can be used to show any given Prolog term in a standard form, with all operators appearing in the functor-and-arguments format. For example, achieving the goal

     ?- display(2 + 3).

will cause

     +(2,3)

to be shown on the screen. Further, achieving

```
?- display(2 + 3 + 4).
```

will cause

```
+(2,+(3,4))
```

to be shown. Try for yourself the following:

```
?- display((g1, g2, g3)).
?- display((g1; g2, g3)).
```

Can you deduce what the codes for the comma and semicolon are? And which has the higher precedence?

To illustrate how the properties of the built-in operators may be set up, here is how the C-Prolog interpreter defines some of its operators.

```
op(1200, xfx,  :-)
op(1200,  fx,  ?-)
op(1100, xfy,  ; )
op(1000, xfy,  , )
op( 900,  fy, not)
op( 900,  fy, spy)
op( 700, xfx,  = )
op( 700, xfx,  is)
op( 700, xfx,  ==)
op( 700, xfx, =..)
op( 700, xfx,  > )
op( 700, xfx,  < )
op( 700, xfx,  >=)
op( 700, xfx,  =<)
op( 500, yfx,  + )
op( 500, yfx,  - )
op( 500,  fx,  - )
op( 400, yfx,  * )
op( 400, yfx,  / )
op( 400, yfx,  //)
op( 300, xfx, mod)
op( 200, xfy,  ^ )
```

How can the user define an operator? Answer: by giving as a goal to the interpreter an instance of the **op** predicate with appropriate arguments. The name of the operator must be an atom. For example

117

```
?- op(100, xfy, '#').
```

This in itself says nothing about the meaning of the new operator or the use to which it will be put. It ensures that from here on the interpreter will recognise structures written in the forms (say)

```
X # Y,

cain # abel,

44 # 53 # 149.
```

The actual use of the operator # will then be up to the programmer, who may wish to give facts and rules involving it, thus regarding it as a *predicate*. Alternatively, # might be intended for use as a data structure former, so that (say)

```
2 # 3
```

is to be regarded merely as an ordered pair of numbers.

20 Examples

This chapter consists of some descriptions of programming tasks. They are grouped according to the kind of task or the kind of data structure involved. Some are short and uncomplicated, and others are more substantial. The last three sections contain individual, larger scale, tasks. The next chapter consists of solutions in the form of Prolog code. The purpose of this is twofold. First, to provide exercises for the reader and second, to provide samples of code which illustrate ideas and techniques.

1. Lists

1. X is a member of the list L.

2. L is the result of concatenating lists L1 and L2.

3. E is the last member of the (non-empty) list L.

4. L1 is the result of reversing the order of the members of the list L.

5. L1 is the result of deleting all occurrences of the object X from the list L.

6. L1 has the same members as L, but with all repetitions removed.

7. Given a list L integers, L1 is obtained from L by multiplying every member of L by 3.

8. Given a string S of lower-case letters, S1 is the string of corresponding upper-case letters.

9. String S1 is a substring of string S2. (The members of S1 all occur in S2, and in the same order, but not necessarily consecutively.)

10. Let us describe as a *table* a list, each member of which is a list containing two members: first an atom and second a number, such that no atom is paired separately with two different numbers. Task: given an atom A and a table T, N is the number which is paired with A in the table T.

119

2. Order

1. S is the smallest member of the (non-empty) list L of integers.

2. S is the largest member of the (non-empty) list L of integers.

3. Given a list L of integers which is ordered by magnitude, L1 is the result of inserting the integer X in the correct place in L.

4. Given non-empty strings S1 and S2 of lower-case alphabetic characters, S1 precedes S2 in dictionary order.

5. Given atoms A1 and A2 (containing only lower-case alphabetic characters, say), A1 precedes A2 in dictionary order. (Hint: use name.)

6. Given a table T as in Example 1.10, with entries ordered alphabetically according to the atoms, T1 is the result of inserting the pair [A,N] in the correct place (A being an atom and N being a number). Note that we may not insert this pair if a pair containing the atom A already occurs in T.

7. A date may be represented by a structure of the form

   date(Day,Month,Year)

   where Day and Year are numbers, and Month is an atom (e.g. 'July'). Task: Given dates D1 and D2, D1 precedes D2.

8. A time of day may be represented by a structure of the form

   time(Hour,Minute)

   Task: Given times T1 and T2 (assumed to be on the same day), T1 precedes T2.

9. Given times T1 and T2 as in the preceding example (T1 is assumed to be before, possibly on the day before, T2), S is the number of minutes between them.

10. Given a table T containing [Date,Atom] pairs (similar to the structure described in Example 1.10), ordered according to the date, T1 is the result of inserting the pair [D,A] into T in the correct place (D is a date, as in Example 2.7, and A is an atom).

3. Sorting

1. Insertion sort (using Example 2.3). L1 is the result of ordering the integers in the list L in increasing order of magnitude.

2. Insertion sort (using Example 2.5). Given a list L of (alphabetic) atoms, L1 is the result of ordering them in dictionary order.

3. Quicksort. Repeat the preceding two examples, but using the quick-sort algorithm rather than insertion sort. Assume that the initial list contains no repetitions. (Outline of the algorithm: denote by H the first member of the given list; find the list S of all members of the given list which are smaller than H, and the list L of all those which are larger than H; recursively quicksort both S and L; concatenate the results, with H placed between them.)

4. See Example 7.4 for a sorting predicate which has a parameter allow-ing the actual order required to be specified (e.g. increasing, decreas-ing, alphabetical, dictionary, etc).

4. Binary Trees

Binary trees of data items can be represented in Prolog, using lists, as follows:

[] represents the empty tree.

[A,Tleft,Tright] represents the tree with data item A at the root, and with subtrees Tleft and Tright.

For example, the tree

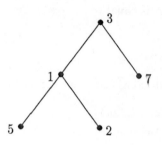

would be represented as

```
[3,[1,[5,[],[]],[2,[],[]]],[7,[],[]]].
```

1. Given a binary tree T, L is a list of all the data items held at nodes of the tree (tree traversal).

2. Think of alternative ways of doing the preceding example, so as to yield different orderings of the data items held in the tree.

3. D is the depth of the binary tree T (i.e. the length of the longest branch).

4. Given a binary tree T with (the ASCII code of) one lower-case character held at each node, T1 is the tree obtained by replacing each lower-case character by the corresponding upper-case character.

5. The binary tree T of integers is ordered, i.e. for every node of the tree, all integers in the left subtree are smaller than the integer at the node, and all integers in the right subtree are greater than the integer at the node.

6. Given an ordered binary tree T (as in Example 4.5 above), T1 is the ordered tree obtained by inserting the integer N at a new leaf node in T in the appropriate position.

7. Given a list L of distinct integers (not necessarily in order), T is an ordered binary tree containing all of the members of L (binary sequence search tree).

8. Treesort. Given a list L of distinct integers, L1 is a list containing the members of L in increasing order. First form a binary tree as in Example 4.7 above, and then traverse it in an appropriate fashion (see Example 4.2) to yield the ordered list L1.

9. T1 is a subtree of T2. This may be easier if we take 'is a subtree of' to include the case 'is equal to'.

5. The Database

1. Suppose that the database contains facts of the forms

```
person_age(Name,Age).
person_sex(Name,Sex).
```

where `Sex` may take value `male` or `female`. Assert into the database additional facts of the form

        person_full(Name,Age,Sex).

one for each person who has both an age record and a sex record.

In the Examples 2 - 7 it is assumed that there is a database containing facts of the form

    mark(Name,Number).

as in one of the examples in Chapter 5.

2. L is a list of all the names appearing in the `mark` facts. (This is similar to the example of `assemblechildren` in Chapter 15.)

3. Transform every `mark` fact by changing all of the marks using the scaling formula

    M + (50 - M)/10.

(using integer division).

4. S is the name of the student who obtained the highest mark.

5. Display all names and marks in descending order of marks.

6. Repeat Example 5.5 but displaying the names and marks in alphabetical order of names (see Example 2.5).

7. Sort the `mark` facts in the database into increasing order of marks.

In the next three examples it is assumed that there is a database containing facts of the form

    train(Origin,Destination,Deptime,Arrtime).

where place names are atoms and clock times are represented by structures as in Example 2.8.

8. Add to the database by asserting into it, for each pair of places which are the origin and destination of some known train, one fact of the form

        shortest(Place1,Place2,Journeytime).

where `Journeytime` is the time for the shortest known journey from `Place1` to `Place2`.

9. Prompt for the required information, and assert a new `train` fact, making sure that no duplication of facts occurs.

10. Prompt for the required information and retract an existing `train` fact (giving an appropriate error message if there is no fact matching the given information).

6. Input/Output

1. Prompt for and input a list of atoms (to be input as a single list structure), sort the list alphabetically (see Example 3.2), and display the atoms in order, one per line.

2. In the context of Example 5.8 above, prompt for and input two places (atoms) P1 and P2, and display on the screen details of all trains from P1 to P2, giving departure and arrival times for each, in an appropriate format.

3. Display on the screen the pattern

4. Given that the database contains facts of the forms

```
grid(X,Y,nought).
grid(X,Y,cross).
```

which represent an arrangement of noughts and crosses on a three-by-three grid as in the preceding example (the X and Y have values from 1 to 3), display the grid with its contents.

5. Manage the input and recording of individual moves in a game of noughts and crosses (tic-tac-toe), including the checking of validity and display of the new grid. This omits the more difficult task of managing the sequence of moves and checking to see whether the game has been won or has finished in a tie, which may be regarded as an exercise.

6. Consult a file F1 containing `mark` facts (as described in Section 5), transform every fact as in Example 5.3, and store the amended facts in a file F2 (using `listing`).

7. Given a file **F** containing Prolog terms (in readable form, i.e. each followed by a full stop and a non-printing character, as described in Chapter 14), the first term in the file being an integer — a count of the number of subsequent terms in the file, display the contents of **F** (other than the count) on the screen.

8. Repeat the previous example, but instead of displaying on the screen, copy to another file **F2** one term at a time, including the count, and making sure that the new file is subsequently readable.

9. Given two files containing integers (in readable form, as in Example 6.7 above) in increasing order, merge the contents of the two files into a single ordered file.

10. Given a file **F** containing text, display the contents of **F** on the screen with all lower-case letters changed into the corresponding upper-case letters and all other characters unchanged.

11. Given a file **F** containing text, to display a message saying whether the character with ASCII code **N** occurs in **F**.

12. Given a file **F** containing text, and an integer **N** in the range 0..127, the character with code **N** occurs in **F**. (This differs from the previous example, in that this predicate will succeed or fail, depending on the case.)

13. Given a file **F** containing text, to find whether the characters with codes **M** and **N** occur together in this order.

7. Structures

1. Prompt for the name of a person (an atom), a date (with three components, as in Example 2.7) and whether a birth or a death is to be recorded, and assert an appropriate **birth** or **death** fact into the database.

2. A class is divided into three groups, and the database contains facts of the forms

```
group1(Name).
group2(Name).
group3(Name).
```

Prompt for a number (1, 2 or 3) and display on the screen all the names in that group.

3. Given a file containing facts of the form

    `student(Name,Number).`

    consult this file, allocate names to groups 1, 2 and 3 cyclically by constructing records `group1(Name)`, `group2(Name)` and `group3(Name)`, and then save these as facts in a file, using `listing`.

4. Insertion sort (general). A predicate may determine an order — examples are `>` and `<`, and the various other orderings mentioned in Section 2 above. Write an insertion sort predicate which has an extra argument, to carry the name of the ordering predicate which is to be used. (See Example 3.4.)

5. (See Example 5.1.) Write a predicate with three arguments, standing for the names of predicates, the intended effect being as follows. The first two arguments are names of predicates for which there are facts held in the database, and the third argument is the name of the predicate which represents the *join* of the first two, and for which facts are to be inserted in the database. Assume that the first argument holds the common values (as with `person_age` and `person_sex` in Example 5.1). Assume initially also that the predicates in question have two arguments. Then generalise to cover the case where they may have any number of arguments, the numbers being given as arguments to the `join` predicate.

8. Menu

Display a menu, prompt for a choice and call an appropriate predicate, in a loop, for the following situation. We have a database containing a diary, consisting of facts of the form

    `engagement(Date,Time,Description).`

(For representations of dates and times, see Examples 2.7 and 2.8.) The options to be provided are:

add : Add a new engagement to the diary.

cancel : Cancel an engagement from the diary.

lookup : Display the engagements for a given day.

tidy : Read in the current date and retract all entries in the diary which are now in the past.

quit : Terminate the session (saving the diary in a file).

This exercise is about the menu, not about the details of the execution of the options, so these may just be represented by predicates with an appropriate form, without corresponding definitions. Important features are the calling of the options, looping back to the menu where required, and a mechanism for exit from this loop.

9. Network Representation

A network has nodes and directional links between nodes. Let us represent nodes by atoms **n1**, **n2**, etc. We may then represent the existence of a link from (say) **n7** to **n3** by a Prolog fact

        link(n7,n3).

Thus a network may be represented by a collection of such facts.

Assume first that we have a network with *no loops*, i.e. it is not possible anywhere in the network to follow a path which leads back to the starting point.

Task1 There is a path from node **M** to node **N**.

Think about the reason for supposing that there were no loops. Now let us allow the existence of loops. And let us use the word *path* to mean a sequence of nodes (no node occurring more than once), in which each node is directly linked to the next.

Task2 There is a path from node **M** to node **N** which passes through none of the nodes in the list **L**.

We may think of **L** as the list of nodes on the path traversed so far, and use this in a recursive predicate which finds paths while avoiding looping paths. Now reconsider the previous task. We can specify it slightly differently:

Task3 The list of nodes **P** is a path from node **M** to node **N**.

Next, let us change the **link** facts so that they contain more information. Say

        link(n7,n3,100).

represents the fact that there is a link from n7 to n3 with 'capacity' (in some sense) 100. It is sensible then to say that the capacity of a path is the smallest of the capacities of the links in it.

Task4 The list of nodes **P** is a path from node **M** to node **N** which has capacity at least **C**.

10. Decision Tree

The value for tax purposes of a company car in the U.K. depends on the original cost of the car, the age of the car and the cubic capacity of the engine. The rules which applied in 1987 are expressed in the table below.

original cost($£$)	age(years)	engine capacity(cc)	value($£$)
$< 19,250$	< 4	≤ 1400	525
		≤ 2000	700
		> 2000	1100
	≥ 4	≤ 1400	350
		≤ 2000	470
		> 2000	725
$19,250 - 29,000$	< 4	any	1450
	≥ 4	any	970
$> 29,000$	< 4	any	2300
	≥ 4	any	1530

Further, the value is halved if the car is used for more than 18,000 miles on business in the year, and has 50% added to it if the business mileage is less than 2,500.

Write a Prolog program which will successively ask the user for the required information for a particular vehicle, and will in due course display the appropriate value for tax. Make sure that the user is asked only for *relevant* information.

21 Solutions

Below are samples of Prolog code, corresponding to the Examples listed in Chapter 20. Before looking at these, the reader should consider the following remarks. As with all programming, there will be alternative approaches to problems, and alternative solutions will result, so the solutions presented here should not be considered as definitive. Second, one learns a programming language by using it, and recourse to a model solution is no substitute for working out the problems for oneself. On the other hand, however, one also learns by seeing examples of code which show standard ways of doing standard things. Each individual should try to balance these factors. In any event, this chapter is not intended merely to be *read* — it should either be worked through or used for reference. Partly for this reason (namely that it should not be too easy to read), and partly for reasons of space, the code presented here is deficient in one important aspect. It lacks sufficient comments. Despite this, the examples should be comprehensible, with due application. In some cases the solution given has been chosen with clarity in mind, where a shorter, more efficient or more elegant solution might have been found. Throughout, solutions have made use of predicates defined in solutions to earlier examples.

1. Lists

1. ```
member(X,[X|_]).
member(X,[_|T]) :- member(X,T).
/**/
```

2. ```
append([],L,L).
append([A|L1],L2,[A|L3]) :- append(L1,L2,L3).
/****************************************************/
```

3. ```
last([E],E).
last([_|T],E) :- last(T,E).
/**/
```

4. ```
reverse([],[]).
```

```
    reverse([H|T],L1) :-
            reverse(T,U), append(U,[H],L1).   /* 1.2 */
    /*****************************************************/

5. del_occs(X,[],[]).
   del_occs(X,[X|T],L1) :- del_occs(X,T,L1), !.
   del_occs(X,[H|T],[H|T1]) :- del_occs(X,T,T1).
   /*****************************************************/

6. del_rpts([],[]).
   del_rpts([H|T],L1) :-
            member(H,T), del_rpts(T,L1), !.   /* 1.1 */
   del_rpts([H|T],[H|T1]) :- del_rpts(T,T1).
   /*****************************************************/

7. triple([],[]).
   triple([H|T],[H1|T1]) :- H1 is H*3, triple(T,T1).
   /*****************************************************/

8. lower_to_upper([],[]).
   lower_to_upper([H|T],[H1|T1]) :-
            H1 is H - 32, lower_to_upper(T,T1).
   /*****************************************************/

9. substring([],_).
   substring([H|S],[H|T]) :- substring(S,T).
   substring(S,[H|T]) :- substring(S,T).
   /*****************************************************/

10. lookup([[A,N]|T],A,N) :- !.
    lookup([[B,M]|T],A,N) :- lookup(T,A,N).
    /*****************************************************/
```

2. Order

```
1. least([S],S).
   least([H|T],S) :- least(T,S1), smaller(H,S1,S).

   smaller(A,B,A) :- A =< B.
   smaller(A,B,B) :- B < A.
   /*****************************************************/

2. greatest([S],S).
   greatest([H|T],S) :- greatest(T,S1), larger(H,S1,S).
```

```
    larger(A,B,A) :- A >= B.
    larger(A,B,B) :- B > A.
    /****************************************************/

3.  insertinorder(X,[],[X]).
    insertinorder(X,[H|T],[X,H|T]) :- X =< H.
    insertinorder(X,[H|T],[H|T1]) :-
            X > H, insertinorder(X,T,T1).
    /****************************************************/

4.  precedes([],[_|_]).            /* Why do we need this? */
    precedes([A|_],[B|_]) :- A < B.
    precedes([C|S],[C|T]) :- precedes(S,T).
    /****************************************************/

5.  dict_order(A1,A2) :-
            name(A1,S1), name(A2,S2), precedes(S1,S2).
    /****************************************************/

6.  /* Compare with 2.3 above */
    pair_insert(P,[],[P]).
    pair_insert([A,N],[[A,M]|T],_) :-
            write('Atom already in the table.'),
            fail.
    pair_insert([A,N],[[B,M]|T],[[A,N],[B,M]|T]) :-
            dict_order(A,B).
    pair_insert([A,N],[[B,M]|T],[[B,M]|T1]) :-
            dict_order(B,A),
            pair_insert([A,N],T,T1).
    /****************************************************/

7.  d_earlier(date(D1,M1,Y1),date(D2,M2,Y2)) :- Y1 < Y2.
    d_earlier(date(D1,M1,Y),date(D2,M2,Y)) :- m_ord(M1,M2).
    d_earlier(date(D1,M,Y),date(D2,M,Y)) :- D1 < D2.

    m_ord(M1,M2) :-
            month_num(M1,N1), month_num(M2,N2), N1 < N2.

    month_num('January',1).
    month_num('February',2).
    month_num('March',3).
    month_num('April',4).
    month_num('May',5).
```

131

```
          month_num('June',6).
          month_num('July',7).
          month_num('August',8).
          month_num('September',9).
          month_num('October',10).
          month_num('November',11).
          month_num('December',12).
          /*****************************************************/

      8.  t_earlier(time(H1,M1),time(H2,M2)) :- H1 < H2.
          t_earlier(time(H,M1),time(H,M2)) :- M1 < M2.
          /*****************************************************/


      9.  time_diff(T,T,0).
          time_diff(T1,T2,Mins) :-
                  t_earlier(T1,T2),    /* 2.8 */
                  interval(T1,T2,Mins).
          time_diff(T1,T2,Mins) :-
                  t_earlier(T2,T1), interval(T2,T1,Mins1),
                  Mins is 24*60 - Mins1.

          interval(time(H1,M1),time(H2,M2),Mins) :-
                  T1 is H1*60 + M1, T2 is H2*60 + M2,
                  Mins is T2 - T1.
          /*****************************************************/

      10. /* Compare with 2.6 above */
          diary_insert(P,[],[P]).
          diary_insert([D,A],[[D,A1]|T],_) :-
                  write('Already engaged that day.'), fail.
          diary_insert([D,A],[[E,B]|T],[[D,A],[E,B]|T]) :-
                  d_earlier(D,E).  /* 2.7 */
          diary_insert([D,A],[[E,B]|T],[[E,B]|T1]) :-
                  d_earlier(E,D), diary_insert([D,A],T,T1).
          /*****************************************************/
```

3. Sorting

```
      1.  isort([],[]).
          isort([H|T],L1) :-
                  isort(T,T1), insertinorder(H,T1,L1).  /* 2.3 */
          /*****************************************************/
```

```
2. dict_sort([],[]).
   dict_sort([A|T],L1) :-
           dict_sort(T,T1), dict_insert(A,T1,L1).

   dict_insert(A,[],[A]).
   dict_insert(A,[B|T],[A,B|T]) :-
           dict_order(A,B).  /* 2.5 */
   dict_insert(A,[B|T],[B|T1]) :-
           dict_order(B,A), dict_insert(A,T,T1).
   /*****************************************************/

3. qsort([],[]).
   qsort([X|T],L1) :-
           separate(X,T,Lowlist,Highlist),
           qsort(Lowlist,LL), qsort(Highlist,HH),
           append(LL,[X|HH],L1).  /* 1.2 */

   separate(_,[],[],[]).
   separate(X,[A|R],[A|Rl],Rh) :-
           A < X, separate(X,R,Rl,Rh).
   separate(X,[A|R],Rl,[A|Rh]) :-
           A >= X, separate(X,R,Rl,Rh).
   /*****************************************************/
```

4. Binary Trees

```
1. traverse([],[]).
   traverse([X,Tl,Tr],L) :-
           traverse(Tl,L1), traverse(Tr,L2),
           append(L1,[X|L2],L).  /* 1.2 */
   /* (symmetric order traversal) */
   /*****************************************************/
```

2. Replace the subgoal append(L1,[X|L2],L) by either

```
append([X|L1],L2,L)
/* prefix walk */
```

or

```
append(L1,L2,L3), append(L3,[X],L)
/* suffix walk */
/*****************************************************/
```

```
3. depth([],0).
   depth([X,Tl,Tr],D) :-
           depth(Tl,D1), depth(Tr,D2),
           larger(D1,D2,D3),
           D is 1 + D3.   /* 2.2 */
   /*****************************************************/

4. translate([],[]).
   translate([C,Tl,Tr],[C1,Ul,Ur]) :-
           C1 is C - 32,
           translate(Tl,Ul), translate(Tr,Ur).
   /*****************************************************/

5. ordered([]).
   ordered([X,Tl,Tr]) :- ord_m([X,Tl,Tr],_,_).

   ord_m([X,[],[]],X,X) :- !.
   ord_m([X,[],Tr],X,H) :-
           ord_m(Tr,Lr,H), X < Lr, !.
   ord_m([X,Tl,[]],L,X) :-
           ord_m(Tl,L,H1), X > H1, !.
   ord_m([X,Tl,Tr],Ll,Hr) :-
           ord_m(Tl,Ll,H1), X > H1,
           ord_m(Tr,Lr,Hr), X < Lr.
   /*****************************************************/

6. insertintree(X,[],[X,[],[]]).
   insertintree(X,[A,Tl,Tr],[A,Ul,Tr]) :-
           X < A, insertintree(X,Tl,Ul).
   insertintree(X,[A,Tl,Tr],[A,Tl,Ur]) :-
           X > A, insertintree(X,Tr,Ur).
   /*****************************************************/

7. build_bsst([],[]).
   build_bsst([H|T],Tree) :-
           build_bsst(T,Tree1),
           insertintree(H,Tree1,Tree).   /* 4.6 */
   /*****************************************************/

8. treesort([],[]).
   treesort(L,L1) :-
           build_bsst(L,T), traverse(T,L1).   /* 4.7 */
   /* (using symmetric order traversal, from 4.1) */
   /*****************************************************/
```

```
9. subtree([],_).
   subtree([A,Tl,Tr],[A,Ul,Ur]) :-
           subtree(Tl,Ul), subtree(Tr,Ur).
   subtree([A,Tl,Tr],[B,Ul,Ur]) :-
           subtree([A,Tl,Tr],Ul); /*semicolon*/
           subtree([A,Tr,Tl],Ur).
   /****************************************************/
```

5. The Database

```
1. join_age_sex :-
           person_age(Name,Age),
           person_sex(Name,Sex),
           assert(person_full(Name,Age,Sex)),
           fail.
   join_age_sex :- write('Records have been joined.').
   /****************************************************/
```

```
2. assemblenames(L) :- makenamelist([],L).

   makenamelist(S,L) :-
           retract(mark(N,M)), !,
           makenamelist([N|S],L),
           asserta(mark(N,M)).
   makenamelist(L,L).
   /****************************************************/
```

```
3. scale_marks :-
           retract(mark(N,M)), !,
           M1 is M + (50 - M)//10,
           scale_marks,
           asserta(mark(N,M1)).
   scale_marks.
   /****************************************************/
```

```
4. best_student(S) :-
           best_mark(M), mark(S,M), !.

   best_mark(M) :- mark(_,First), best(First,M).

   best(Bestsofar,M) :-
           mark(_,X), X > Bestsofar, best(X,M).
```

```
        best(M,M).
        /***************************************************/


5.  marks_list :-
            best_mark(M),
            retract(mark(N,M)), !,
            write(M), tab(4), write(N), nl,
            marks_list,
            asserta(mark(N,M)).
    marks_list.
    /***************************************************/


6.  alpha_list :-
            first_student(N),
            retract(mark(N,M)), !,
            write(N), tab(4), write(M), nl,
            alpha_list,
            asserta(mark(N,M)).
    alpha_list.

    first_student(S) :-
            mark(Name,_), first(Name,S).

    first(Firstsofar,N) :-
            mark(X,_),
            dict_order(X,Firstsofar),
            first(X,N).
    first(N,N).
    /***************************************************/


7.  order_by_marks :-
            best_mark(M),
            retract(mark(N,M)), !,
            order_by_marks,
            assertz(mark(N,M)).
    order_by_marks.
    /***************************************************/


8.  best_trains :-
            train(P1,P2,_,_),
            not(shortest(P1,P2,_)),
            get_best_time(P1,P2,T),
            assert(shortest(P1,P2,T)),
```

136

```
                fail.
        best_trains.

        get_best_time(P1,P2,T) :-
                train(P1,P2,Dep,Arr),
                time_diff(Dep,Arr,Time),   /* 2.9 */
                best_time(P1,P2,Time,T), !.

        best_time(P1,P2,Sh_sofar,T) :-
                train(P1,P2,S,F),
                time_diff(S,F,TT),
                TT < Sh_sofar,
                best_time(P1,P2,TT,T).
        best_time(P1,P2,T,T).
        /***************************************************/

  9. add_train :-
                enterdetails(P1,P2,Dep,Arr),
                not(train(P1,P2,Dep,Arr)),
                assert(train(P1,P2,Dep,Arr)),
                write('The new train has been added.'), !.
        add_train :- write('This train is already listed.').

        enterdetails(P1,P2,Dep,Arr) :-
                write('Enter details of train:'), nl, nl,
                write('Origin:        '), read(P1),
                write('Destination:  '), read(P2),
                write('Departure time (24-hr clock): '),
                read_time(Dep),
                write('Arrival time (24-hr clock):   '),
                read_time(Arr).

        read_time(Time) :-
                repeat, read(T), convert_time(T,Time), !.

        convert_time(T,time(H,M)) :-
                M is T mod 100, M < 60,
                H is T//100, H < 24, !.

        convert_time(_,_) :-
                write('Error in input of time.'), nl,
                write('Please enter it again:       '), nl,
```

```
              fail.
/*****************************************************/

10.  remove_train :-
              enterdetails(P1,P2,Dep,Arr),   /* 5.9 */
              retract(train(P1,P2,Dep,Arr)),
              write('The train has been removed.'), !.
     remove_train :- write('This train is unknown.').
/*****************************************************/
```

6. Input/Output

```
1. atom_sort :-
              write('Enter a list of atoms,'), nl,
              write('separated by commas, and'), nl,
              write('enclosed in square brackets:'), nl,
              read(L),
              dict_sort(L,L1),   /* 3.2 */
              write_list(L1).

     write_list([]).
     write_list([H|T]) :- write(H), nl, write_list(T).
/*****************************************************/

2. show_trains :-
              enter_places(P1,P2), nl, nl,
              display_heading(P1,P2),
              train(P1,P2,Dep,Arr),
              tab(2), t_write(Dep), tab(6), t_write(Arr),
              nl, fail.
     show_trains :-
              nl, write('End of list of trains.'), nl.

     enter_places(P1,P2) :-
              write('PROLOG TRAIN TIMETABLE'), nl,
              write('----------------------'), nl, nl,
              write('Enter departure point: '), read(P1),
              write('Enter arrival point:   '), read(P2).

     display_heading(P1,P2) :-
              write('Trains from '), write(P1),
              write(' to '), write(P2), nl,
```

```
                  write(' are as follows:'), nl, nl,
                  write('Departure  Arrival'), nl,
                  write('---------  -------'), nl, nl.

    t_write(time(H,M)) :- write_2(H), write_2(M).

    write_2(0) :- write('00').
    write_2(N) :- N > 0, N < 10, write('0'), write(N).
    write_2(N) :- N >= 10, write(N).
    /**************************************************/

3. grid_display :-
                  nl, nl,
                  blank_row, horiz_line,
                  blank_row, horiz_line,
                  blank_row, nl, nl.

    blank_row :- tab(23), write('|    |'), nl.

    horiz_line :- tab(20), write('-----------'), nl.
    /**************************************************/

4. game_display :-
                  nl, nl,
                  tab(21), write_row(1,1), horiz_line, /* 6.3 */
                  tab(21), write_row(1,2), horiz_line,
                  tab(21), write_row(1,3), nl.

    write_row(3,Y) :- get_entry(3,Y,E), put(E), nl.
    write_row(X,Y) :-
                  get_entry(X,Y,E), put(E),
                  write(' | '), NewX is X + 1,
                  write_row(NewX,Y), !.

    get_entry(X,Y,88) :- grid(X,Y,cross), !.
    get_entry(X,Y,48) :- grid(X,Y,nought), !.
    get_entry(X,Y,32).
    /**************************************************/

5. play(P) :-
                  read_move(P,X,Y),
                  record_move(P,X,Y),
                  game_display.  /* 6.4 */
```

```prolog
read_move(P,X,Y) :-
        repeat,
        write('Place '), write(P), write(' at'), nl,
        write('coordinate X (1,2 or 3): '), read(X),
        write('coordinate Y (1,2 or 3): '), read(Y),
        check_move(X,Y).

check_move(X,Y) :- not(grid(X,Y,_)).
check_move(X,Y) :-
        write('Illegal move. Try again.'), nl, fail.

record_move(P,X,Y) :- assert(grid(X,Y,P)).
/***************************************************/
```

6. ```prolog
   scale_and_file :-
           consult(marks),
           scale_marks,  /* 5.3 */
           tell(newmarks), listing(mark), told.
   /***************************************************/
   ```

7. ```prolog
   display_file(F) :-
           see(F), read(Count), copy(Count), seen.

   copy(0).
   copy(N) :-
           read(X), write(X), nl,
           M is N - 1, copy(M).
   /***************************************************/
   ```

8. ```prolog
   copy_file(F1,F2) :-
           see(F1), tell(F2),
           read(Count), write(Count), put(46), nl,
           rcopy(Count),
           seen, told.

   rcopy(0).
   rcopy(N) :-
           read(X), write(X), put(46), nl,
           M is N - 1, rcopy(M).
   /***************************************************/
   ```

9. ```prolog
   merge_files(F1,F2,F3) :-
   ```

```
                get_pair(F1,C1,F2,C2),  /* get counts */
                get_pair(F1,A,F2,B),
                tell(F3),
                C is C1 + C2, writeterm(C),
                M is C1 - 1, N is C2 - 1,
                n_merge(A,F1,M,B,F2,N),
                told.

        get_pair(F,X,G,Y) :-
                see(F), read(X),
                see(G), read(Y).


        n_merge(A,F1,M,B,F2,0) :-
                B =< A, writeterm(B), writeterm(A),
                see(F1), rcopy(M), seen,  /* 6.8 */
                see(F2), seen.  /* close F2 */
        n_merge(A,F1,0,B,F2,N) :-
                A =< B, writeterm(A), writeterm(B),
                see(F2), rcopy(N), seen,
                see(F1), seen.  /* close F1 */
        n_merge(A,F1,M,B,F2,N) :-
                A =< B, writeterm(A),
                see(F1), read(AA), MM is M - 1,
                n_merge(AA,F1,MM,B,F2,N).
        n_merge(A,F1,M,B,F2,N) :-
                B < A, writeterm(B),
                see(F2), read(BB), NN is N - 1,
                n_merge(A,F1,M,BB,F2,NN).

        writeterm(T) :- write(T), put(46), nl.
        /****************************************************/


10. caps(F1,F2) :-
                see(F1), tell(F2),
                repeat,
                get0(X), modify(X,Y), put(Y),
                X = 26,  /* end of file */
                told, seen.

        modify(X,Y) :- X > 96, X < 123, Y is X - 32, !.
        modify(X,X).
        /****************************************************/
```

```
11. char_search(F,N) :-
            see(F),
            repeat, get0(X), test(X,N),
            seen.

    test(N,N) :-
            write('Character '), write(N),
            write(' occurs in the file.'), nl.
    test(26,N) :-              /* end of file */
            write('Character '), write(N),
            write(' does not occur in the file.'), nl.
    /**************************************************/

12. occurs_in(F,N) :-
            see(F), try_find(N,Found), seen, !,
            Found = true.

    try_find(N,Found) :-
            repeat, get0(X), decide(X,N,Found).

    decide(N,N,true).
    decide(26,N,false).
    /**************************************************/

13. together(F,M,N) :-
            see(F),
            try_find(M,Foundm),   /* 6.12 */
            check_next(Foundm,N,Foundn), !, seen,
            Foundn = true.

    check_next(true,N,Foundn) :-
            get0(X), decide(X,N,Foundn).  /* 6.12 */
    check_next(false,_,false).
    /**************************************************/
```

7. Structures

```
1. record_event :-
            write('Enter name (atom): '), read(P),
            write('Enter date -'), nl,
            write('       day: '), read(D),
            write('       month: '), read(M),
```

```prolog
          write('        year: '), read(Y),
          write('birth or death? '), read(E),
          S =.. [E,P,date(D,M,Y)],
          assert(S).
  /****************************************************/

2. group_names :-
          write('Enter group number: '), read(N),
          group(N,G),
          S =.. [G,Name], call(S),
          write(Name), nl,
          fail.
  group_names :- write('End of list.').

  group(1,group1).
  group(2,group2).
  group(3,group3).
  /****************************************************/

3. allocate :-
          consult(studentfile),
          put_in_groups(1),
          tell(gfile1), listing(group1), told,
          tell(gfile2), listing(group2), told,
          tell(gfile3), listing(group3), told,
          write('Group allocation complete.').

  put_in_groups(4) :- put_in_groups(1).
  put_in_groups(C) :-
          retract(student(N,_)),
          group(C,G),
          S =.. [G,N], assert(S),
          CC is C + 1,
          put_in_groups(CC).
  put_in_groups(_).
  /****************************************************/

4. gen_sort(_,[],[]).
  gen_sort(Ord,[H|T],L1) :-
          gen_sort(Ord,T,T1),
          gen_insert(Ord,H,T1,L1).

  gen_insert(Ord,X,[],[X]).
```

```
      gen_insert(Ord,X,[H|T],[X,H|T]) :-
              P =.. [Ord,X,H], call(P).
      gen_insert(Ord,X,[H|T],[H|T1]) :-
              Q =.. [Ord,H,X], call(Q),
              gen_insert(Ord,X,T,T1).
      /* Think about the case when X = H */
      /****************************************************/

  5. join(A1,A2,A3) :-
              S1 =.. [A1,K,X], S2 =.. [A2,K,Y],
              call(S1), call(S2),
              S3 =.. [A3,K,X,Y],
              assert(S3),
              fail.
      join(_,_,_) :- write('Join created.').
      /****************************************************/


      gen_join(A1,N1,A2,N2,A3) :-
              functor(S1,A1,N1), functor(S2,A2,N2),
              get_args(S1,N1,[K|L1]),
              get_args(S2,N2,[K|L2]),
              call(S1), call(S2),
              append(L1,L2,L),   /* 1.2 */
              S3 =.. [A3,K|L],
              assert(S3),
              fail.
      gen_join(_,_,_,_,_) :- write('Join created.').

      get_args(S,N,L) :- find_args(S,N,0,[],L).

      find_args(S,N,N,L,L).
      find_args(S,N,M,T,L) :-
              MM is M + 1, arg(MM,S,X),
              append(T,[X],T1),
              find_args(S,N,MM,T1,L).
      /****************************************************/
```

8. Menu

```
/****************************************************/
diary :-
      display_menu,
```

```
        choice(C),
        call(C),
        (C = quit; diary).

choice(C) :-
        repeat,
        write('Enter your choice: '),
        read(C),
        available(C), !.

available(add).
available(cancel).
available(lookup).
available(tidy).
available(quit).

quit :- nl, write('GOODBYE !'), nl.
/* add, cancel, lookup and tidy require definitions */

display_menu :-
        nl, write('PROLOG DIARY'), nl,
        write('------------'), nl, nl,
        write('The following operations'),
        write(' are available.'),
        nl, nl,
        write('1. Add a new engagement (add.).'), nl,
        write('2. Cancel an engagement (cancel.).'), nl,
        write('3. Show the engagements'),
        write(' for a day (lookup.).'), nl,
        write('4. Remove all past'),
        write(' engagements (tidy.).'), nl,
        write('5. Terminate the session (quit.).'),
        nl, nl.
/***********************************************************/
```

In the above, the loop is recursive. The goal `call(C)` must always succeed. An alternative formulation of the recursion could rather have recursive calls to `diary` at the ends of the rules for the predicates `add`, `cancel`, `lookup` and `tidy`, but not `quit`.

The loop could also be formulated using `repeat`, as follows.

```
/***********************************************************/
diary :-
```

```
        repeat,
        display_menu,
        choice(C),
        call(C),
        C = quit.
/**********************************************************/
```

9. Network Representation

```
connected(N,N).
connected(M,N) :- link(M,X), connected(X,N).
/**********************************************************/

avoid_path(_,N,N).
avoid_path(L,M,N) :-
        link(M,X), not(member(X,L)),   /* 1.1 */
        avoid_path([M|L],X,N).
/**********************************************************/

path(M,N,P) :- find_path([M],N,P).

find_path([N|T],N,P) :- reverse([N|T],P), !.   /* 1.4 */
find_path([H|T],N,P) :-
        link(H,X), not(member(X,T)),
        find_path([X,H|T],N,P).
/**********************************************************/

ok_path(M,N,C,P) :- find_ok_path([M],N,C,P).

find_ok_path([N|T],N,C,P) :- reverse([N|T],P), !.
find_ok_path([H|T],N,C,P) :-
        link(H,X,C1), not(member(X,T)),
        C1 >= C,
        find_ok_path([X,H|T],N,C,P).
/**********************************************************/
```

10. Decision Tree

```
company_car :-
        get_cost(C), get_age(A),
        find_val(C,A,V),
```

```prolog
        adjust_val(V,V1),
        nl, write('Value for tax is (pounds): '),
        write(V1).

get_cost(C) :- nl, write('Enter original cost of '),
        write('the car (in pounds): '), read(C).

get_age(A) :- nl, write('Enter the age of '),
        write('the car (in years): '), read(A).

find_val(C,A,V) :-
        low_cost(C), get_size(S), low_val(A,S,V).
find_val(C,A,V) :- mid_cost(C), mid_val(A,V).
find_val(C,A,V) :- high_cost(C), high_val(A,V).

get_size(S) :- nl, write('Enter the engine size of '),
        write('the car (in cc): '), read(S).

low_val(A,S,V) :- young(A), young_low_val(S,V).
low_val(A,S,V) :- old(A), old_low_val(S,V).

mid_val(A,V) :- young(A), value(7,V).
mid_val(A,V) :- old(A), value(8,V).

high_val(A,V) :- young(A), value(9,V).
high_val(A,V) :- old(A), value(10,V).

young_low_val(S,V) :- small(S), value(1,V).
young_low_val(S,V) :- med(S), value(2,V).
young_low_val(S,V) :- large(S), value(3,V).

old_low_val(S,V) :- small(S), value(4,V).
old_low_val(S,V) :- med(S), value(5,V).
old_low_val(S,V) :- large(S), value(6,V).

adjust_val(V,V1) :-
        high_limit(H),
        nl, write('Is the business mileage more than '),
        write(H), write('? (y./n.) '), read(Ans),
        Ans = y, V1 is V/2, !.
adjust_val(V,V1) :-
        low_limit(L),
```

```prolog
          nl, write('Is the business mileage less than '),
          write(L), write('? (y./n.) '), read(Ans),
          Ans = y, V1 is V*3/2, !.
adjust_val(V,V).

/* And now for the explicit values and criteria: */

low_cost(C) :- C < 19250.
mid_cost(C) :- C >= 19250, C =< 29000.
high_cost(C) :- C > 29000.


young(A) :- A < 4.
old(A) :- A >= 4.

small(S) :- S =< 1400.
med(S) :- S > 1400, S =< 2000.
large(S) :- S > 2000.

high_limit(18000).
low_limit(2500).

value(1,525).
value(2,700).
value(3,1100).
value(4,350).
value(5,470).
value(6,725).
value(7,1450).
value(8,970).
value(9,2300).
value(10,1530).
/**********************************************************/
```

Appendix A   Built-in Facilities

Most of the following are the forms taken by goals. Details are given of the circumstances in which such goals will succeed, or of the side effects which they cause, or both. The parameters denoted by upper case letters may in general be Prolog terms of any kind, or, indeed, may be variables. Where indication is given of the nature of these parameters in particular cases, it should be understood that in practice a goal is always given in the context of certain instantiations of variables. What is important is the nature of the parameters after such instantiations have been made.

The mark **R** which appears against some entries is to indicate which of the built-in predicates can be re-satisfied on backtracking. Notice that there are very few of these. In particular, it is important to remember that the input and output predicates are satisfied only once, and are passed over (not re-satisfied) on backtracking.

The list given here may not be a complete list for your particular Prolog system. Interpreters vary, and some variations are described below, but in order to avoid confusion the list contains only what might be regarded as the basic standard facilities. One particular area where the differences are great is the debugging tools provided, and it is for this reason that only a few of these are described in detail below.

Remember that the predicates described here are system-defined. The interpreter will object if you attempt to re-define any of them.

abolish(X,Y)

Removes from the database all clauses for the predicate with name **X** and number of arguments **Y**. Not available on some systems.

abort

Causes all current executions to be terminated, and a return to the top-level interpreter, irrespective of the current depth of nested breaks. See **break**.

arg(X,Y,Z)

The X-th argument in the structure Y is Z. X and Y must be instantiated. E.g.
`?- arg(2,father(adam,cain),Z).`
will cause the instantiation Z = cain.

assert(X)

Adds the clause X, which may be either a fact or a rule, to the database. This is normally the same as `assertz(X)`. E.g.
`?- assert((old(X) :- age(X,Y), Y > 30)).`
`?- assert(age(john,63)).`

asserta(X)

Inserts the clause X into the database at the beginning.

assertz(X)

Inserts the clause X into the database at the end.

atom(X)

X is (or is currently instantiated to) an atom.

atomic(X)

X is (or is currently instantiated to) an atom or an integer.

break

Suspends execution by the interpreter, and starts up another Prolog interpreter. This interpreter operates with the same database, but otherwise is independent of the suspended interpreter. When this second-level call has been completed (by CTRL-Z or otherwise), the suspended execution is resumed. It is possible to nest **break**. Some systems give an indication of the current level of nesting. See **abort**. For a fuller description, see also Chapter 18.

call(X)   **R**

It is sometimes convenient in a program to have a variable standing for a goal, and then to give that goal to the interpreter to be satisfied. `call(X)`, given as a goal, asks the interpreter to try to satisfy X. X may be any Prolog term, but normally will be a variable, which of course has to be instantiated to a term which may be interpreted as a goal.

`clause(X,Y)`   **R**

When this is given as a goal, the interpreter will seek to find a clause in the database with head matching X and body matching Y. X must be instantiated enough so that the predicate in the head of the clause is known.

`consult(X)`

Causes the transfer of facts, rules and goals from the file X. X must be an atom. Facts and rules are asserted into the database and goals are satisfied (or not) in the normal way during the consult. If X is an atom, giving the goal ?- [X]. at the terminal has the same effect as ?- consult(X). If X is a list of atoms (filenames), then all the files in the list will be consulted.

`debugging`

Lists all current spy points.

`display(X)`

Causes X to be written to the current output with all operators shown as prefix operators.

`fail`

A goal which fails immediately, causing backtracking.

`functor(X,Y,Z)`

X is a structure whose functor is Y and which has number of arguments Z. In normal use, X will be instantiated initially, and satisfying this goal will cause Y and Z to become instantiated.

`get(X)`

Causes X to be instantiated to the (ASCII code for) the next printing character read from the current input. Non-printing characters are lost. X must be a variable.

`get0(X)`

Causes X to be instantiated to the (ASCII code for) the next character read from the current input. When it reaches an end-of-file, get0 returns (the code for) CTRL-Z. X must be a variable.

`integer(X)`

Succeeds if X is (or is currently instantiated to) an integer.

`is(X,Y)`

X is the value of the arithmetic expression Y. This is normally used in the infix form X **is** Y. Its purpose is normally to instantiate X.

`length(X,Y)`

Y is the length of the list X. Normally used to instantiate Y, i.e. to compute the length.

`listing(X)`

Sends to the current output (screen or file) a listing of all clauses in which X occurs as the functor in the head. X must be an atom.

`name(X,Y)`

Y is the list of (ASCII codes for) the characters which form the atom X. Either argument may be uninstantiated initially.

`nl`

Causes the next output to be placed on a new line.

`nodebug`

Causes all spy points to be removed.

`nonvar(X)`

Succeeds if X is not a variable.

`nospy(X)`

Removes spy points. See the entry below for **spy** for details of the form of X. Note that **nospy** is an operator, and so may be used without parentheses, e.g. ?- **nospy** X.

`not(X)`

A goal which succeeds if and only if the goal X fails.

`notrace`

Switches off tracing.

number(X)

Succeeds if X is (or is currently instantiated to) a number.

op(X,Y,Z)

Declares an atom Z as an operator with type Y and precedence X. See Chapter 19.

put(X)

Causes the character whose ASCII code is X to be sent to the current output. X must be an integer in the appropriate range.

read(X)

Causes X to be instantiated to a Prolog term read from the current input. The term must be followed by a full stop and a new line or a space. Note that terms of any size or complexity can be read by means of a single read(X) goal.

reconsult(X)

As consult, but clauses from the file X supersede existing ones for the same predicate, all of which are lost. At the terminal, reconsult(X) may be abbreviated by list notation, e.g. ?- [$marks]. Another symbol may be used on your system in place of the $. It could be ~ or -. Note that ?- [$user]. is possible.

repeat   R

A goal which immediately succeeds, and can be re-satisfied infinitely often on backtracking.

retract(X)   R

Removes from the database the first clause which matches with X. Note that X need not be fully instantiated, and that satisfying a retract in such circumstances will not only remove a clause (if there is one which can be matched), but may also cause instantiations which can be used in subsequent subgoals.

retractall(X)

Removes from the database all clauses which match with X. On some systems it may cause the removal of every clause whose head matches with X. See also abolish.

see(X)

Switches the current input so that subsequent input is read from the file X. X must be (or be instantiated to) an atom. Input can be switched without the previously open file being closed. If X is not already open, it is opened at the beginning. See Chapter 14.

seeing(X)

Causes X to be instantiated to the name of the file which is currently the one associated with the input.

seen

Closes the current input file and causes subsequent input to be taken from the terminal (unless switched by another **see** goal, of course).

skip(X)

Reads (and ignores) characters until the character (whose ASCII code is) X appears. X must be an integer in the appropriate range.

spy(X)

Sets a spy point on all clauses for X. X may be an atom (the name of a predicate) or an atom followed by a number (the number of arguments), or a list of these. The form varies on different interpreters. E.g. spy(age), spy(age(2)), spy(age/2), spy([age,old]). Note that **spy** is an operator,and may be used without parentheses, e.g. ?- **spy age**. During execution, whenever a spy point is reached, the user is prompted to choose from several options which may help in debugging.

tab(X)

Causes X spaces to be sent to the current output. Remember that this gives relative, not absolute, tabulation.

tell(X)

Switches the current output so that subsequent output is written to the file X. X must be (or be instantiated to) an atom. Output can be switched without the previously open file being closed. If the file X is not already open, it is opened (created if necessary) at the beginning. See Chapter 14.

telling(X)

Causes X to be instantiated to the name of the file which is currently associated with the output.

told

Closes the current output file and causes subsequent output to be written to the terminal screen (unless switched by another **tell** goal, of course).

trace

Switches on tracing.

true

A goal which succeeds immediately (and, unlike **repeat**, is not re-satisfied on backtracking).

var(X)

Succeeds if X is an uninstantiated variable.

write(X)

Causes the term X to be written to the current output. If the term is (or contains) an atom enclosed in single quotes, the quotes are not written.

writeq(X)

As **write(X)**, except that atoms enclosed in single quotes are written with the quotes. Not available on all interpreters. See Chapter 14.

_   (underscore)

The anonymous variable. This matches with anything, but is never instantiated.

!

Cut. This is explained in detail in Chapter 13.

X, Y

Conjunction of goals ('and').

`X; Y`

Disjunction of goals ('or').

`X = Y`

Succeeds if term `X` can be matched with term `Y`.

`X == Y`

Succeeds if term `X` is identical (as a Prolog term) with term `Y`.

`X =:= Y`

Succeeds if the values of the arithmetic expressions `X` and `Y` are equal.

`X \= Y`

The same as `not(X = Y)`. Not available on some interpreters.

`X \== Y`

The same as `not(X == Y)`.

`X =\= Y`

The same as `not(X =:= Y)`.

`X < Y`

The arithmetic expression `X` evaluates to a number which is smaller than the value of the arithmetic expression `Y`.

`X > Y`
`X =< Y`
`X >= Y`

Comparison of arithmetic values, as for `<`.

`X + Y`

Sum. Remember that arithmetic expressions are not numbers. If their values are required, the predicate **is** must be used.

`X - Y`

Difference.

`X * Y`

Product.

`X ^ Y`

Raise to a power.

`X / Y`

Quotient. On systems without floating point numbers, this means integer division.

`X // Y`

This stands for integer division on systems where the symbol `/` is used for (floating point) division.

`X mod Y`

Integer remainder.

`sqrt(X)`

Square root.

`exp(X)`

Exponential.

`log(X)`
`log10(X)`

Logarithms, natural and base 10.

`sin(X)`
`cos(X)`
`tan(X)`

Trigonometric functions: sine, cosine, tangent.

`asin(X)`
`acos(X)`
`atan(X)`

Inverse trigonometric functions: arc sine, arc cosine, arc tangent.

`[X1, ... ,Xn]`

The list with `X1`, ...,`Xn` as members.

[X|Y]

The list with head X and tail Y.

[X,Y|Z]

The list with first member X, second member Y, with Z as the remainder. This notation can be extended, e.g. [A,B,C,D|T].

[]

The empty list.

.(X,Y)

The list with head X and tail Y. On some systems this must be written '.'(X,Y). The '.' may on some systems be an infix operator, allowing the notation X . Y.

X =.. Y

X is a structure and Y is a list whose head is the functor in X and whose tail consists of the arguments in X. If X is a specific structure, then this can be used to instantiate Y. If Y is a list whose head is an atom, this can be used to instantiate X to an appropriate structure.

/* ... */

Used to delineate comments. All characters between /* and */ are ignored by the interpreter.

Appendix B   ASCII Character Codes

The codes for all of the printable characters are given (in decimal) in the table below.

33	!	49	1	65	A	81	Q	97	a	113	q
34	"	50	2	66	B	82	R	98	b	114	r
35	#	51	3	67	C	83	S	99	c	115	s
36	$	52	4	68	D	84	T	100	d	116	t
37	%	53	5	69	E	85	U	101	e	117	u
38	&	54	6	70	F	86	V	102	f	118	v
39	'	55	7	71	G	87	W	103	g	119	w
40	(	56	8	72	H	88	X	104	h	120	x
41	)	57	9	73	I	89	Y	105	i	121	y
42	*	58	:	74	J	90	Z	106	j	122	z
43	+	59	;	75	K	91	[	107	k	123	{
44	,	60	<	76	L	92	\	108	l	124	|
45	-	61	=	77	M	93	]	109	m	125	}
46	.	62	>	78	N	94	^	110	n	126	~
47	/	63	?	79	O	95	_	111	o		
48	0	64	@	80	P	96	`	112	p		

Other codes are: 13 (carriage return), 26 (end-of-file) and 32 (space).

Index

Index